Looking for Love with All the Wrong Husbands

"I" Manual

Tee Fuller

WESTBOW
PRESS®
A DIVISION OF THOMAS NELSON
& ZONDERVAN

WestBow Press books may be ordered through booksellers or by contacting:

WestBow Press
A Division of Thomas Nelson & Zondervan
1663 Liberty Drive
Bloomington, IN 47403
www.westbowpress.com
1 (866) 928-1240

ISBN: 978-1-4908-8442-4 (sc)
ISBN: 978-1-4908-8444-8 (hc)
ISBN: 978-1-4908-8440-0 (e)

Library of Congress Control Number: 2015909561

Print information available on the last page.

WestBow Press rev. date: 7/22/2015

Scriptures taken from www.BibleGateway.com unless otherwise noted.

Contents

Introduction

Today's the day I begin, and I'm so excited … finally, finally. Although I'm thrilled to start on this journey with you, I have to admit it's very daunting. Years of my life are just sitting before me, waiting. I have printed out my notes, rallied up all the random pieces of paper, and arranged them into little messy stacks around my office. You see, it seems like I've always had this obsession about writing down what I believed to be spiritually noteworthy. I wanted nothing to be lost in thought, so down it would go with some type of writing device on some type of paper product.

As I stand in my office, glancing around at my collected works, my mind is trying to process how important they are. But I feel an underlying stir, and it's as if these pieces of paper all have minds of their own and they've already made their choices as to where they want to fit.

The words the Lord has brought to me, the hope He's planted in my heart, and the revelation of His love for me all need to be included. It's my desire this will offer up comfort to you and me. We will know that it's all been for something. I pray all this disarray will be incorporated into a volume that holds encouragement, hope, support, and worth.

You see, this story, this manual, is about me. I understand that in the end I will have laid before you my personal life—the good, the bad, and the horrible. I'm not going to even try to hide the fact that this is somewhat scary for me and a little overwhelming. But I know the Lord is definitely in this and has been urging me on, showing me this is not only right but the right time. Inside my head I keep hearing, "Tell your story. Just tell your story." So that's what I'm going to do.

Early on I made a decision not to include any personal names. My method is not to get you caught up in personal association with my characters. I'd rather utilize them to bring you into my life of wrong choices and show the healing of a life gone awry.

Along the way you'll be able to pick out my peculiar habits and identify my decisions. My resolution for this story was that I be open and write as I talk and feel. It's very important that my words are me, the real me. One example of that methodology is the fact I don't capitalize the name of satan (unless it begins a sentence). I realize that's not the correct way, but it's my way. I don't underestimate him as an opponent, and I pray you don't either. But I also don't want to give him any misguided notion that I'm paying homage to his name. Instead I prefer to use the word *enemy*. This word offers me the ability to talk about the devil and also group in the fallen angels. I do, however, always capitalize the name of God, and when I use the term *Him* or *You* (in direct address), meaning God, I always capitalize that too.

This manual could have been recounted and framed as a sad story—it could have been a story of a pitiful woman who never bothered to get out of the pit she'd dug for herself. But it's not. It's a story of a young girl who grew up in a Christian family with parents, sisters, friends, boyfriends, and husbands. It's a story that demonstrates what can happen when you don't prepare, with the Lord, for events designed to take you on a pathway clearly not marked as yours.

My manual reveals the truth, and it's not pitiful. It's awesome. It's not sad. It's glorious. It's not broken. It's firmly planted. The truth is that even before my birth, God deposited within me an available and long-lasting relationship with Him, and He determined a path for me to follow. Through the years I untied a few of those cords that held me close to Him. Just like an old fairy tale, those crumbs, those dropped crumbs and bits and pieces of life, are what helped me to find my way back to Him, back into safety. They brought me back under His wings. They brought me to this place.

> He will cover you with his feathers, and under his wings you will find refuge; his faithfulness will be your shield and rampart.
>
> —Psalm 91:4 NIV

Chapter

1

The Beginning

So many people don't like to drive and would be fine if they could take public transportation everywhere, but I'm not one of them. One of my loves is getting in the car and turning on either Christian music or Christian talk radio. I can separate myself from the hustle and bustle of daily living and go where I want to go and listen to what I choose.

As I began my trip, I immediately flipped through the stations, looking for one playing a song I could sing. If I couldn't find one of those, I'd switch over to a talk show, and back and forth I'd go. Invariably, at some point during the ride, I'd hear one of the speakers mention a particular subject or maybe just say a word that would catch my attention. However, I was never prepared to capture it. If I did have a pen, it was either stashed in the glove box, in the backseat, deep in my purse, or hiding under all the other things in the console. So I'd begin searching with one hand for something to use. When paper wasn't available, I wrote on grocery receipts, paper plates, and backs of appointment cards. These incredible, almost unreadable paper notes were jotted down not only with pens but with eyebrow pencils, lipstick liners, and, yes, even a crayon. Embarrassingly I confess that several times I even wrote on my bare leg when I could find no paper product.

One of the stories my older sister told anyone who would listen was about the day she went to my car to look for something. She opened the passenger door, bent down to look on the floor, and saw a bundle of clothes behind the driver's seat. When she lifted the clothes, she realized something metal was underneath them. That's when she found the waffle iron. Now, mind you—it wasn't in a box, and it wasn't a present. It was just a used waffle iron in my car. She loved telling that story, and each time she did, she'd add another ridiculous element and another new facial expression. I even heard her say one day that when she opened it up, there was still a waffle in it. I admit that, yes, I used to be a car slob, and I did have a waffle iron in my car. But it did not have a waffle inside. Even though I've thought and thought about it, I just can't come up with an excuse or a plausible reason the waffle iron lived in my car, so I'll just let my sister's story live on.

I do think being an overpacker was always one of the biggest contributors to that problem. I never knew when to stop. I'd start with a small suitcase and then begin to calculate how much it would hold. I'd instantly doubt it was big enough, and that's when I'd launch into a debate with myself about whether to take a larger one. My brain signaled me to grab the bigger suitcase because of my incessant need to always be prepared for anything and everything. But then I'd think how bulky one large suitcase would be and start contemplating the benefits of taking two medium ones. By that time, I was in way over my head.

The entire time my mind debated these points, I was figuring out everything necessary to pack. Eventually I'd pull out the two medium suitcases and put my regular clothing in one and pack the extra stuff into the other. I mean, who knew what kind of horrible mess I might find myself in? I might get stuck somewhere and have to spend more days than I planned. I also wasn't going to discount my age-old problem of never knowing whether tomorrow would be my skinny clothes day or my fat clothes day. So to help myself out, I put in everything.

Another contributor to my car issue was where I lived. My home was about forty minutes from my church and the nearest town. So anytime I left, I had to take everything I needed for everyone I'd see and for all my appointments. So if you had asked my friends and relatives about this situation, they'd say my problem wasn't due to not being prepared; it was because I was super prepared.

There really was a method to my madness, and it did start out as what I like to call a clean mess. So after my admission of guilt as a rather obsessive traveler and car hoarder, you may have a better understanding of why it was difficult to actually put my hand on paper and pen.

When I try to think back to the very beginning of all these paper pieces of my life, I'm reminded of how most of them became players. I'd watch Christian programs on television, and many of these scattered notes were taken down right as those on the programs were speaking. There were no iPhones or remotes with function keys for recording or going backward to retrieve what had been said. You either got it or you missed it. Believe me—trying to write what they said while trying to listen to what they were saying was very difficult.

But you know, all the notes, grocery receipts, and little ragtag pieces of paper held costly and worthy evidence of God's love and promises. To tell you the truth, I didn't know early in the game why I seemed to have this obsession with writing things down. At some point I hoped all these papers would eventually take on personalities of their own and come together to reveal something important.

So while I am standing in my office, looking over this somewhat organized chaos, I have to admit these scraps of paper don't look like any library of knowledge or an area that would even hold truth and wisdom. The stacks are ragged because of the variety of writing material I used and it certainly doesn't inspire trust in whoever may be responsible for their keeping. It actually looks more like there was a little eruption and the bits and pieces fell into something akin to piles. But I know what's on these pieces of paper. I know the struggles and hopes contained within them, and I choose to see them as future promises of expectation.

Chapter
2

New Friends

In 2007, I excitedly began to plan an early retirement from my position with a state agency. My dream was to have a good income and do whatever I wanted whenever I wanted. I never felt a burning desire to be extremely wealthy, but I wanted to have enough money to enjoy my life and be able to help others. In the months prior to my actual retirement, my mind frequently wandered. Peaceful thoughts of resting, sleeping in, watching daytime television, and vacationing in seclusion came into view.

It was my understanding retired people had tons of time to pick and choose what they wanted to do, and I was actually worried I might become bored. Little did I know what was coming. Soon after I retired, I discovered an evil twin was going out, wearing my face, and volunteering me to bake, cook, feed, type, sing, travel, babysit, and fill any job left vacant. Only later did I realize this evil twin was actually me choosing what I thought I wanted to occupy my life.

After my stretch of voluntary bondage I realized I needed to sort through and prioritize my life. I didn't want to just be busy. I wanted my life to be full. I also wanted to be in charge of picking good options. I put together a mental job description to keep myself a little more in line because that way I could accomplish more in the areas I wanted to be involved in.

I also had a huge desire to move away from the town I worked in for so long. I'd poured so much of my life into that job that I felt if I could get away from the nearness of it, I would be able to breathe again. I was ready for a huge change and eager to move forward. A tourist town in the foothills of eastern California became our new home. There were lots of antique shops, and the town's overall attitude was very slow-moving, for which I was thankful.

Shortly after the move my niece introduced me to a married Christian couple I instantly liked. The wife worked in the medical field, and the husband was involved in music ministry. His work hours varied, so he occasionally came to our house for coffee, and we talked about spiritual stuff. At that time I was married to Husband #4, but for quite some time I'd contemplated my need for at least a permanent separation. As my friendship with this couple grew, I saw firsthand a good Christian marriage. I asked them how they were able to do it after thirty-five years of marriage. Their answer was they had agreed divorce was never to be an option for them. They also prayed together and sought the Lord together.

One afternoon while he was waiting for his wife to join us, my new friend began to speak to me about finding my place with God. My marriage was a mess, and I was a mess. Really I wasn't prepared at all to try to figure out what he was sharing with me, but that never stopped him. I look back now and realize he was a mature enough Christian to know that if I repeatedly heard the truth, I'd eventually catch on, and at that time God could bring revelation into my life. I'm sure he knew that when I finally got it, when I finally figured it out, I'd hold it in my heart and allow it to change me and then pass it on.

My friendship with this couple remains to this day, and I am so thoroughly grateful for the time they spent in prayer over me and the wisdom they allowed themselves to share. I think I'm most grateful because I know it was not only a labor of love but a beginning as well. I'd listen to him talk while I tried to take simple notes, attempting to remember just how he would say things. I wanted to get just the right words in the right places because I knew truth would be found in the correctness of those words. In self-defense, I also learned I had to have something more than a few paper towels and an eyebrow pencil to write with. Even though he would see me taking notes, he never slowed down. He said what came into his mind as it came to him. Eventually I discovered I would hear it again, and at that time I would have the luxury of making changes. So as our talks continued, so did my paper collection. I didn't know enough about what he was telling me to be able to assimilate it, so I just kept gathering and gathering.

I remember one particular day when my friend added something new by stating that God could be to me whatever I needed Him to be. I had not ever heard anyone say anything like that. I immediately remember feeling as if that was like taking the awesome greatness of God and demoting Him, so I just shook my head and wondered what he could really be saying. I didn't mention anything to him that day, but over the next couple of weeks he repeated it, and it probably took me close to six months to finally even get a glimpse of a possibility of knowing what he was trying to toss my way.

But hearing something and only having a very basic knowledge of it doesn't mean you're ready to operate in it. At that point I still had no real concept about how to let go and have a greater personal and trusting relationship with the Lord in my life. I'd always prayed, believed, and loved Jesus, but my friend was trying to help me understand I needed to fully trust, fiercely believe, and then totally surrender to my Lord.

It took several years before I began to comprehend and relate to the full depth of his statement about God being to me what I needed Him to be. One day it just popped into my head, and I knew I had just received a huge revelation from the Holy Spirit. It wasn't relegating God to a lower standing. It was just me allowing, believing, and expecting my God to meet me in my times of trials and tribulations. It was me trusting and knowing my God would present Himself, no matter the position I asked Him to play.

Many things my friend shared with me were new concepts. I wanted to keep them and hold them in my heart and my memory, and I wanted to find out what they really held for me. So it continued, all my happenings and all my findings, all noted on my paper pieces of life.

Chapter
3

Just Scraps

I have fond memories of one of my random pieces, scribbled on a
cheap paper plate that was folded in half. I easily remember where
I was and what I was doing. I was driving in my car to a lunch
meeting and listening to the radio when I heard a woman talking
about spiritual warfare in women. It was all based on 1 Samuel 17,
which is about David and Goliath. She began to explain how David's
belief in God's authority and power enabled him to slay Goliath with
only a slingshot. She went on to say women could find confidence,
determination, victory, and contentment in their lives if they would
persevere in letting God fight their battle. It immediately drew my
attention, and I knew I had to get down all the key points. I was
in an area where I couldn't pull over, so I frantically reached into
my brown paper lunch bag and pulled out my paper plate. After
clumsily folding it in half I started writing while it rested on my
knee. I couldn't look down, so the end result is pretty unattractive,
but when done, there was promise and inspiration on that paper
plate. I still have it, it's still folded in half and still holds information

that became significantly useful in my life. That's why it's one of my valued paper pieces.

As in the beginning of anything in life, those scraps of paper held incomplete thoughts and lots and lots of questions. Just like you, no matter the start, that scrap gets tossed around and can become tattered. It may even have some little pieces missing, but still wanting to become beautiful and rather remarkable. Through the godly process of becoming remarkable, that scrap will take on truth, forgiveness, strength, joy, and love. As God has taken my scraps of paper and helped me to make sense out of them, He'll do the same for you. He'll take you from the beginning, all incomplete and messed up with missing pieces, and He'll sort you, tidy you up, and give you guidance until you're on your way. What He inspires me to give life to in print He will inspire you to live out on the path that He has set before you.

Chapter
4

Truth of Process

At this moment while I am sitting down to write this manual, I would venture to say that I'm in the middle of a new start. It's much like a weeding out process, but the Lord has persuaded me that now is my time. Every so often I'd get this stirring in my gut, like a restlessness, and I'd walk into my office and want so badly to begin to piece together and sort out everything. Bringing together all my notes, the research, and all the bits and pieces of what had taken me so long to gather was an enormous undertaking. So as usual, I'd get that same overwhelming feeling, which up to that point had always trumped my want, and I'd turn around and walk right back out.

I hadn't used file folders, and I didn't want my significant pieces of information to stay hidden inside my computer. I wanted to be able to get to them easily. Stuffing them away would have been like putting them all into hiding without allowing them their rightful place. They needed to be available for me to glean the precious insight contained within them. They had to be available with all the others, waiting to be chosen.

So each time I walked in prepared to do battle, I'd find myself walking back out without starting, and then I would get this awful feeling of personal dissatisfaction. I mentioned earlier that this was a daunting task and that it's taken quite a long time to get started, but I'm beginning to understand God's timing in all of this. I realize now I had to be ready. I had to be devoted and willing. I had to learn to listen to the Holy Spirit. I had to be healed.

Much of my desire to listen for God came from my new Christian friend who sowed seeds of truth into my life for several years. Many times in leaving our talks, he'd look directly into my face and say, "When you find out how much Jesus really loves you, you won't *need* the love of a man." That statement went way over my head, and I truly had no idea then what he was really talking about. Honestly I absolutely had not one clue.

One morning after one of our get-togethers, my friend made that same remark again, but then he followed it up with an even more bothersome statement. He said, "I see you as if you're on the front of a locomotive speeding down the tracks." Again I didn't really know what he meant, so I shook my head, not wanting to appear stupid. But his words rolled around in my head for hours after he left, and I still didn't have any concept of why he'd chosen those words, but what I did know was that it wasn't good.

At some point it occurred to me that this couple and I had truly become friends and that the Lord had put us together for a reason. She gave me the friendship of another woman, and he was doing double duty as a friend and spiritual mentor. Together they brought to me a stirring within my spirit and an expectation of hope.

When I think back now at some of the questions I asked and some of the statements I made to my friend, I'm uncomfortable and almost embarrassed. Some of the words I chose to say came out of despair, but some came from the issue of not being able to let go of old emotions and beliefs. But my friend never showed disappointment or irritation, and he never walked away, and he never gave up on me. It took many months for me to become bold enough to even consider the options and the truth that he had been trying to get across to me. None of it ever changed the comfortable feeling of our friendship, and it also never changed how much he desired to help me. I had no idea back then just how much influence his words would have in my life.

One day while he was waiting for his wife to join us, my friend mentioned how much he cared for her. He had spoken very little about their personal relationship when she wasn't there to participate, but that day he told me he loved her more than anyone else in this world. That led us into a heavy conversation about the pitfalls of separations and divorces because by that time I was definitely in one. He said it was his belief that if every married man treated his wife the way God had instructed him to in the Bible, there would never be the need for divorce. He genuinely believed that a woman would never feel needy or unloved if her husband gave her the love she was supposed to be given. His belief was that the wife would never have the desire to look outside of marriage for another if her husband put her second only to God. He stated he had faith in the fact that if the husband followed God's plan for marriage, his wife would naturally respond to him with loyalty and respect.

You know, I had never heard a man say anything like that. In truth, I had never even thought a man was capable of thinking that way. Totally leaving out my new friend, all my male family, and my ministers, my thoughts about men were absolutely less than desirable. I had witnessed many men who had shown unworthiness and a lack of self-control as well as an inability to be trusted. To this day I will admit that it was a very long and difficult process for me to even allow myself to think I might have this all wrong. That didn't eventually happen because of me. It happened in spite of me. As time went on, it was the Lord who brought before me examples of families with strong Christian husbands. He did this over a long period of time, and eventually it caused me to begin to watch and wonder. But actual changes in this area and having an open mind about it were really difficult for me. I'd always felt I had proof of my belief in regard to most men, and now God was showing me it was only one page out of thousands. I knew the Lord was in this, so I began to pay attention, and eventually I gave in a whole inch and let a positive yet questioning thought creep in. I realized it was possible that I could be wrong. Maybe it was also just possible that I'd limited myself to a common thread of men.

That process was all about the Lord getting me to believe what He was showing me and about me trusting Him in this. The tough part even now is to admit to the world and myself how really long that took. I feel very blessed that the Lord was so patient in allowing me time for healing and time to accept change.

Chapter
5

Youth—How Sweet It Is

When I look at our family album and see pictures of myself, I realize I looked like who I felt I was inside, a blonde, curly-headed little girl who was shy, sweet, and impressionable. The photo's all showing my same smile with a wide gap in between my two front teeth. Because of the white blonde hair color, you really saw no eyebrows or eyelashes, just two big blue dots for eyes.

By the time I was five, my younger sister would have just been born, and my older sister would have been eight. It was an awesome feeling to have someone in my life that was there already when I was born into the family, and she was mine. I truly confess I was captivated by my older sister. She had dark thick hair while mine was blonde and fine. She was tall and lean while I was shorter and not lean, and her personality was dramatic while mine was reserved. We almost couldn't have been more opposite. She was the leader, and I always followed. Because I was the proverbial pest, I followed her everywhere. I could never quite figure out why we were so different until one afternoon my mom reminded me that my older sister and I had a different dad. My mom pulled out a couple of pictures, and my sister and I looked through them. It became obvious that she took after her natural dad and our mom and I took after my natural dad. That was a strange realization because I had never thought of her as my half sister, just as my sister, but to me it didn't matter. She was still mine.

Our family lived in a middle-class neighborhood in a fairly small town, and most of the kids on my block were girls. Since I was always more the tomboy type, I played outside whenever I could, and as a result, I had a year-round suntan. My parents worked hard to provide for us, but having three daughters proved to be rather expensive. As we grew older, they explained that if we wanted to have extra things, we should use our allowance as well as any other earned money to buy them. I thought that was really a harsh idea because I wasn't interested in earning anything, including my allowance. It was my feeling that I just wouldn't want extra stuff until I remembered if I didn't have an allowance, I couldn't go to the neighborhood store and buy candy.

We always shared inside housework, and our mom was pretty good at dividing up jobs according to our ages. Our house was filled with hardwood floors so every couple of months my mom would wax them. My older sister and I would help by putting socks on our feet and then running and sliding up and down the hallway until the floors shined or until we gave up in exhaustion.

As a young adult I remember thinking my mother had been pretty smart. She'd figured out a way of keeping us out of her hair on the weekends because every time we'd go into the house, she'd say, "Oh, I'm so glad you're here. I've got something I need you to do," and *bam*, you'd have a chore.

But the day my life changed horribly was the day my dad added me to the employment of lawn-mowing duty. I had to mow with a push mower the whole back yard and then edge the patio while my older sister raked leaves and got ready to do the same thing in the front yard.

I hated—not disliked but hated—outside work. My tomboy days included playing in the grass areas, skating, bike riding, and swimming but never digging in the dirt or handling bugs. All outside work always involved both with a little sweating thrown in. But my parents didn't agree with me, so we were raised with our own list of chores, and we were given payment in our very own allowance.

Now as much as I wanted a bike, I knew at my age there was no way I could earn enough money to buy one, so I begged and pleaded for one as a birthday gift. My sister already had hers, but she wasn't really into sharing, even if I could have reached the pedals. One day while I was playing in the garage, my mom and dad surprised me with my very own bike. I was ecstatic. I didn't know how to ride yet, but I knew when I learned, I'd be able to go everywhere my older sister did.

As a youngster, my eyes only saw what I wanted them to see, but in reality, if memory serves me right, it was definitely put together secondhand. The fenders over the wheels weren't just one color. They looked more like a car that had been all buffed out and was ready to be painted. I'm sure the beauty of my most prized possession escaped everyone but me. I thought it was glorious. I rode that thing everywhere, as far and as fast as I could with my ponytail just flying in the wind. I loved it, and it was mine.

One of my favorite places to play was in the garage. The back of the garage door was made up of wooden crossbeams, and that's where I would put my inventory of empty cereal boxes and cans for my pretend store. My mom would help me out by saving for me what she could. I didn't worry about anyone pulling open the garage door because my parents didn't use it for our car; it was being used for a project. My dad was in the process of building a boat, and he and my mom would work on it during their slack time.

One day while I was roaming around and looking for stuff for the store, I spied a large pair of black leather roller skates sitting on a shelf. When I asked my mom who's they were, she said they were my dad's and that he had always loved to skate. Not too long before that, I'd gotten my first pair of metal roller skates, and it was my dad who sat me down on the porch steps and showed me how to tighten them onto my shoes. Then he took me out to the driveway and the sidewalk while he taught me how to skate.

Even after all this time I still remember how much fun we had when our family would go skating at the local skating rink. When my dad thought I was ready, he began teaching me how to dance on skates with him. It was somewhat like what you see when you watch ice skaters on television minus the part about perfection and beauty. Around and around the rink in our dance position, skating backward and making swirls and turns—it was an awesome time between my dad and me, and now it's also an awesome memory.

As I'm sitting here, reminiscing about things that happened a long time ago, I'm remembering something weird that happened one day between my mom and me. My earliest memory of communication didn't involve talking with someone. I just remember singing … anywhere and everywhere.

On this particular occasion I was probably about five, and my mom was cleaning in the bathroom. I was just hanging out with her and playing with something. Because I really didn't know all the words to any song, I would just make up my own, and it probably sounded more like a melody line with accented gibberish. I think my mom had been cleaning for a long time or what seemed like a long time to me, and I'd probably been singing that entire time. I remember her standing at the sink, and she stopped and looked down toward me and then very seriously said, "I didn't know you knew French." There was a moment of time that stood still as I looked up at her, and I remember thinking how silly she was for thinking it was French when I didn't even know French. When I think about that now I realize my mom wasn't being weird. She was just trying to play. That thought puts a big grin on my face because I know as a mom I've done those same silly things, but now I wonder, *Did my kids get it, or did they think I was weird too?*

Somewhere around the age of seven or so, I finally gave in and accepted the fact that my mom wasn't going to give me a brother. I didn't have any close boy cousins, and most of the kids in our neighborhood were girls, so I'd really hoped we'd have one. It's possible I'd been waiting for a playmate because I was so much the tomboy and I wanted someone to play with, someone who played what I liked to play. I wasn't at all feminine like my two sisters, and although my older sister was exceptional in sports and could easily slide into home plate, the rest of the time she was the epitome of striking good looks. However, I wore either braids or a slicked back ponytail, and because my hair was so blonde, the only thing you saw when you looked at me were those big blue eyes, a tanned face, and white teeth with that gap. My shirt was always hanging halfway out. My knees were usually skinned, and I bit my nails.

In third grade the only boys I really got face-to-face with were the ones at school—one of those in particular. There he would be sitting on his bike about fifty feet down from the corner of our block, waiting for me after school. When he would see me at the corner of my street, he'd start pedaling as fast as he could, and when he got close, he'd throw his bike down and start to run toward me. If he could catch me, he'd grab and pull at my long hair and hold onto it while he'd try to kiss me. I'd be trying as hard as I could to kick him, and he'd be trying just as hard to get that kiss. Believe me when I say that was not a good start into my relationship pattern with men.

One afternoon I was rubbing my head where some hair had been pulled out, and I had tears in my eyes. My older sister asked me why I was crying, so I told her my big sob story about what had been happening. I don't think I even realized at that age that I could just tell people my problem and they would actually fix it for me. But fix it she must have because that never happened to me again. I'd walk all the way to the beginning of the corner and stop and then carefully peek down the block, but he wouldn't be there. It's funny. Even after all these years I can still visualize his face and remember his name. She became my hero that day.

My sisters and I held many secrets between us throughout the years, and one of these occurred early in life. We lived in an era when no one worried over their children about them being taken by serial killers or about them being kidnapped and sold into sex slavery. But my parents did have a set of basic safety rules. We were only allowed to leave our block with their permission and always with at least one other person, and we had to be home by dinner or before dark, whichever occurred first. Living in a small town had its advantages. They knew that if one of us did get hurt, we only had to knock on anyone's door, and they would get help.

So with permission my older sister and I would occasionally walk to the community pool, where we'd meet our school friends. She was probably around twelve or thirteen, and according to my mom and dad, she was certainly old enough to be responsible for me. I'm not sure, but I think the pool was at least a mile from our home, so my older sister, being the creative thinker, found a shortcut. All the land surrounding our town was filled with grape vineyards, and it was normal for all the kids to travel through them, eating grapes as we went about our business. Before the pool there were train tracks where the trains would come in and load up the grapes and then leave for various parts of wherever. My sister decided she didn't want to walk all the way around to the crossing, so she taught me how to crawl underneath the trains. She thought it was fun, but I was terrified. As the follower, I had to do it because she'd already be on the other side and she never acted like she was in a mood to wait. She somehow had convinced me that she knew when the trains were loading and moving. Even though I trusted that she knew what she was doing, I should have been suspicious when she made me promise to never tell our mom.

Had my mother ever found out, my sister and I would have been grounded for life and kept from the pool, probably until we had our own children. If my memory serves me right, I think we were in our thirties when we finally decided it was safe to tell her about our many escapades.

As in many families, we sisters were very different from one another. By the time I was in my preteens, my older sister was dating, and my younger sister was close to seven. I was still the tomboy, but my younger sister, much like my older sister, was more feminine and had the darker hair like our mother. In thinking back on our childhood, I realize it must have been difficult for her because I had been so attached to my older sister, and because she was so much younger, sometimes she missed out.

She, however, learned very quickly about all my quirks, and she played that game well. She was very young when she found out I had a thing about feet. I don't like and have never liked feet, even my own. But she would get the biggest kick out of putting her feet on me and then listening to me scream for her to get them off, and then I'd get in trouble for being too loud. It was amazing how such a little person could have become so tricky. It didn't take her long to learn that I'd be willing to give her anything just to get her to quit putting her feet on me. Still to this day I know if given the opportunity and just for any old reason, she'd do it in a heartbeat and then laugh until she cried.

There was a huge difference in the personalities between the three of us, and there were also differences because of our ages. I believe we definitely lived within the pattern relegated to first or eldest child, middle child, and baby or last child. Actually what I'm speaking of is normally referred to as the middle child syndrome. But the really weird thing is that as a youngster I didn't know there was such a thing, but when I got older, I heard someone talk about it one day. I remember thinking, *Yep, that's me. That's my life.*

I've never been the kind of person who used sickness or addictions or even a syndrome as a way to get sympathy or to be used as a reason I wasn't able to change something or even quit something. But that doesn't alter the fact that life happens, and there are results, so you just do your best to cope and try to adapt.

I know there are many people who don't believe in this way of thinking, and to that, I'd like to say that it's probably because you're not a middle child. The middle is rather like how people might interpret tepid water, not hot and not cold. I'm not so much talking about the qualities of the person. I'm speaking more about his or her placement in life.

Now I don't have a degree in behavioral science. I'm just speaking as one who was born not as a first child and not as a last child. But as that middle child, I realize there were times when I would feel as if I was lost in the mix and had a general feeling of being average.

I'm not sure that I didn't experience what a lot of middle children experience, which is the feeling that they have no real, set purpose within the family unit.

In my case that wasn't something that was present in my mind, but inside in there somewhere I think it may have been lingering. I do, however, remember thinking that there were definite advantages to being the older and the youngest of the siblings.

According to a variety of different items I've read over the years, it appears it may be fairly normal for the middle children to believe they're not significant. If you feel as if you're not important or even noteworthy, this definitely allows for a mind-set and a way of thinking that brings forth low self-esteem and insecurity.

It's not my purpose to unload on any parents, including my own. I know my parents tried to do their very best in the raising of their children. I personally believe it's probably common that parents are not consciously aware of the fact that the one in the middle might somewhere get lost along the way. I would venture to say that I didn't have any idea what it was about me that made me feel average or run of the mill and unremarkable. But I think I did feel that way, and because of that, maybe I also presented myself that way.

I'm thankful that my parents taught us to pray, and I'm thankful that our God is deeply concerned about each of us. So please be careful not to let yourself or your spouse or your children get lost in the shuffle of life. Be big in God and be victorious spiritually. Pray with expectation that the Lord will bring to each member of your family the purpose that He placed inside of them. Take care to let each of them know how special they are. They may not know that you think they're special, or they may not want to hear it from you; however, I would tell you that you should say it anyway.

Chapter

6

The Faces of Shame

Many of my childhood memories come back easily, and I've always believed most of them to be worthy of remembering, except one in particular. It was a hidden part of me that I didn't talk about for more than thirty years. It was something I had no control over, and yet it was something so personal I felt overwhelming shame. It didn't involve abuse or anything that actually happened to me. I was just that unlucky girl who lived my young life as a bed-wetter.

What's really odd to me is in saying those words to myself while typing them in this sentence, it seems rather small. It doesn't sound like an experience that was so horrible that it should cause me to hide that part of myself for most of my life. But to me I didn't live it small. I lived it as though it was huge, and its significance in my life was of agonizing humiliation and embarrassment. Still to this day I don't understand any of it, and I continue to work at not feeling as if I was personally devalued because of it. I'm still hesitant for it to be a topic of conversation, and it's still something I would prefer not to discuss. But when I began this manual, I told the Lord I'd be as honest and open about everything as I could be if it would hold any hope in the knowing.

What I do understand is that my secret kept me immobile for a great portion of my youth, and I grew up in a constant state of dread that one of my friends would find out. I would hide it any way I could and from whomever I could. It was only much later in life when I finally verbally admitted it to one person, and then it was only because they had a child with the same problem and the parent was desperately looking for answers.

Growing up in the sixties was tough, and people just assumed if you were that kid, you were probably just lazy. One of their attempts at change would be to deny you anything to drink after six o'clock in the evening. It didn't matter even if your room was on fire. You were not getting water. They tried setting alarms to make sure you got up in the middle of the night, but that wouldn't work either. Although my parents never mistreated me in this area, I remember hearing stories of other kids who didn't have parents like mine, and they took the avenue of spinning guilt. I wished and wished to be normal and for it to go away, and I hated that this portion of my life was out of my control. I held myself responsible even though inside I knew I wasn't. Each morning became a new day to be filled with another disappointment and a new reason to be anxious. There was not a bone in my body that wasn't ashamed, and it became a regular habit to feel inadequate for not being able to fix it. The doctors told my parents there was apparently nothing wrong physically, so in my mind I wondered, *Why?* What was it about me that just wasn't right? Why did it have to be me? I think this was a particularly hard pill for me to swallow because I was that kid who was insecure. This affront to my life just added to the sensation of being all the more separated. All during the day you're doing your best to be that average kid and do all the regular things in life that all the other kids are doing, but at night that's when your life changes.

In youth, even though you know afflictions generally set you apart from others, you're still too young emotionally to realize the extent of it. You don't understand what might happen to you based on your own degree of approval or disapproval of your own self. You certainly can't see the consequences of a life you've already begun filling with blame or shame. As that child, there was no understanding that some things were just beyond my ability to control and that shame and blame should not have been my end result.

I want to say to you that as that child, my parents wouldn't have known what I was going through emotionally because there weren't clear warnings, and I certainly wasn't about to bring it up myself. They just wouldn't have had any concept of what I secretly began to see as myself as I grew older. Why would they ever have considered that this shy, sweet kid would take on guilt and apply humiliation to her life? Maybe some would think I just didn't care or that it hadn't mattered because I held it all inside for years and years and quite frankly, tried to forget it all.

Everything in life was different back then. No one talked openly about difficult events or sexual matters or confusing times. It would have been well beyond our time for parents to wonder what may have been the cause for their children becoming distant or introverted or even easily embarrassed.

I pray this hasn't been your situation, and I pray that your children haven't lived their lives in secret either. Just because they don't volunteer to tell you or just because you can't see it, that doesn't mean hurt, anger, bitterness, shame, loneliness, and confusion aren't part of their daily living. Much of your children's activities are in places and situations away from you. You don't know everything that is spoken to them or even everything that happens to them. Take care to pray over yourself and your family every day, and don't just assume everything is okay. Pray for their protection and for wisdom. My advice is to let your kids know they can come to you with anything they need to say, no matter what, with no condemnation or anyone saying, "I told you so."

Chapter

7

Confidence and Newness

If you're fortunate enough to be a person who has natural confidence, that's great because apparently there's no fear involved in doing what you want to do. Try going for the moment, sweating it out, and thinking if you do this thing, it might make you either throw up or become so afraid that you can't move. When you feel that way, all you can do is stand there and stare with a glazed look on your face. That's how people react when they're truly fearful and lacking in self-confidence.

I knew I wasn't a leader, but as a youngster I didn't see that as a negative. It was just who I was. Because confidence was something I'd never experienced, I didn't even realize it was something I was missing. But later when challenged to stretch myself toward various opportunities, I began to understand that I had wrongly assumed my life was workable just the way it was. Having lived that assumption led me to inadvertently trade what could have become confidence for a type of settling. I missed out on the joy of being carefree, and I missed out on the growth and development of the gifts and ministries the Lord had placed inside of me. As I grew older, I remember lots of times when I would look for dates or partners who had self-confidence because it allowed me to just borrow theirs temporarily. All I had to do then was let them lead, and I'd be able to enjoy whatever was going on as long as they were close or as long as I could hang on to them. I made that be okay and then internally justified my action and tried not to think about it.

It was my singing that gave me such personal gratification, and I longed to be able to share it without having feelings of inadequacy. Not being able to freely sing and enjoy the pleasure of having others receive from it was truly heartrending. I knew the Lord had blessed me with a gift, and gifts from God are intended to be shared. But going through misery each time I tried was awful, disappointingly awful. It caused me to begin a tucking-in and hiding role—you know, the one where you assume if you don't think about it or do it, it'll just go away. Well, we all know how well that works because nothing like that ever just goes away on its own. It just gets tucked in.

I'm a big believer in the theory that some people are born with personalities that aren't normally animated, but I also know in my heart that God always wants you to be confident and never ashamed or fearful. When you allow the enemy to bring in fear and timidity, it causes a negative in your life that God didn't plant there. That fear covers up the person God planned for you to be and totally stunts your progress.

Initially I began life with a shy, naïve type of personality. Allowing fear and guilt and all the other stuff life brought to attach itself to my already reserved existence caused me to develop into someone with no self-worth. I totally lacked in self-esteem, not at all the type of person anyone should want to partner up with.

Remember the enemy has been on earth a long, long time. He's had the opportunity to study your family bloodlines and generational problems within your family members. The enemy listens to your words and watches the reactions you throw out so carelessly. You're the one who provides the further ammunition against your own self. It's easy for the enemy to set traps for you now because now they know your patterns of behavior and they understand your expectations. That coupled with the fact that you live surrounded by a sinful, flesh-filled world makes it super tough to get through life unscathed. It's not impossible to imagine that many youth have never had the pleasure of meeting the Lord in spirit or having a type of relationship that brings them to Him in time of need. But that's exactly what they should do. They should run to Him and ask for help. God's set a plan for your life, and it's to prosper you, give you good health, and give you the desires of your heart. It's the enemy and his fallen angels that will do their best to take you down one disappointment and painful moment at a time.

I had allowed the enemy to present fear and shame to me, and I allowed him to keep those feelings of unworthiness so near in my mind that I felt constrained. I would pray about not being afraid, but it never seemed to actually work. Only now do I understand it was because I always allowed myself to just get afraid again. When presented with fear, I found myself being drawn forward and gravitating toward it. Now I realize the majority of what I'd been doing was just hoping and wishing, but it wasn't actually mixed in with real faith. In regard to my singing, it just was not in me to be bold and sing with the gift God had given me, and I didn't yet have the know-how or the tools to find that faith for myself.

But what I want to tell you at this very moment is that it is never too late with God. No matter what age you are or how badly you've been damaged, those years that have gone by and the dread you feel because you think they're lost, God doesn't recognize as a defeat. When He looks down at you, He sees His royal child. He's crazy in love with you, and He smiles. What He doesn't do is look down at you and say, "If only—" But I had heard my own voice say that.

Chapter
8

First Loves

Our family was very fortunate to have a nice, sweet neighbor who one day asked my mom if I could go to church with her. It wasn't long before my whole family began attending, and that little neighborhood church became our family's home church. One day the minister was talking about what it meant to be saved, and then he followed his sermon up with a question. He asked if there was anyone attending that day who wanted to be saved, and then he said if there were people who wanted to be saved, they should walk forward to him. Well, that sounded good to me, so I jumped up and began to walk forward. When I got to the altar, the minister told me I should ask God to forgive my sins and believe that Jesus died for me. Then I would be saved. By that time I'd heard a lot of Bible stories that included Jesus, and being saved sounded pretty good. At the tender age of almost eight I asked God to forgive me of all my sins, and for me that was that. That was the day Jesus became my first love. Of course at that age I didn't feel any heavy burden being lifted off of me. But I knew about Jesus, and I also knew He was in my life to stay. When I think about it now, it was much like I just tucked Jesus into my heart pocket and went about my young life.

I often think it was because I was saved as a child, it seemed easy for me to believe that my Jesus was who they said He was. I never questioned in my mind whether He heard my prayers, and I never remember thinking about Him not answering them. It was really like I carried Him around with me, like He was just a part of me. I don't remember long sessions of prayers or even talking to Him at length, but I never felt He wasn't there. It was almost as if there was always a connection. Knowing He was with me and in me helped me in my attempt to do what I knew to be right. It was when I started high school that I was confronted with a new set of issues involving problems I'd never had to face before. I was still very shy; however, I had a core group of friends, and we had all gone through elementary school together. We followed one another into junior high and then on to high school.

It was during my junior year that I began dating the quarterback of our football team. By the time of my sixteenth birthday we'd not only dated for a while, we were considered to be going steady. We were always together in school, and when we were out of school, we were on the phone. However, our dating relationship only lasted several more months after that birthday.

One night my parents called me in for a talk and said they had met with my boyfriend's parents that day. This was troubling news to me, and of course it brought an immediate thought of wariness to my mind. I couldn't think of anything that would have prompted that talk, but no matter what it had been, I knew this was not going to be good.

Apparently the talk had been about the depth of the relationship between me and my boyfriend. My parents said that the feelings we'd expressed to each other during these teen years could only lead to trouble.

My parents didn't ask me anything, and they didn't leave any room open for questions. From that moment on, we were both absolutely forbidden to see each other, go on dates, exchange phone calls, or even receive letters. Well, I didn't know how strict other parents were in other families, but I did know how strict mine were. If they'd made a decision that he couldn't be in my life, I knew it was all over (save for the shouting).

I wasn't able to talk to him so the situation at school was really difficult. I cried off and on all day, and of course all my friends wanted to know what had happened. They couldn't ask him because he hadn't shown up for school. I wanted so badly to talk and possibly make future arrangements for contact, but that never happened. There were no cell phones to use and no Internet to contact him with, and our parents were much too smart to allow us to go through our friends. It was just over in a matter of minutes. My life as I knew it was over, or so it seemed.

I'd always been that kid who tried to follow the rules and obey my parents. I was curious, but I tried not to step out too far from the rules. But in this situation it was just too difficult. It had happened too fast, and it was too permanent. Up to the moment of our talk I had believed this was the guy I was going to marry and live with all my life. But when my parents made a decision together, they were immovable. It was so challenging because I wanted to follow what they asked me to do, but I was just caught up in my own distress and sadness. I was no different than any other teenage girl with a broken heart.

I just knew this separation from him in my life was going to leave my heart crushed and my spirit defeated. I thoroughly questioned what was happening and why they hadn't let us say good-bye to each other.

One day I vividly remember walking around our house and just looking for a dark place to be by myself. I ended up lying on our couch, sobbing and praying at the same time. I cried until I couldn't cry anymore, and that's when I told the Lord I really didn't think I was going to be able to get through it. It was just too hard, and it was too much of a hurt.

I remember just crying and pleading with Him. At that point I didn't know what I expected God to do. All I knew was that I needed His help, and I needed to be able to just come out with my feelings and tell Him all about it. I'd never faced a challenge like that, and it certainly wasn't something I'd been prepared for. Nor could I fix it.

All I could think was that I had to know something. Would I have him back someday, or did I need him to just be gone from my life? The uncertainty of the reason, the fact that there hadn't been a final talk or even a good-bye left a heavy feeling in my heart. So right then I made a decision that if God showed me this wasn't the person He had for me in my future, then I'd let it go, but if he was, if God could show me he was, I'd hold on and keep myself somehow together while I waited.

I didn't second-guess myself. I didn't wonder if God would answer me, and I didn't worry if I could believe Him when He did answer. I honestly didn't give any thought to any of that. I just prayed because my heart was broken and I needed to know. God's answer came within three days. I went to school just as if everything was normal, and one of my friends came up and told me he had moved away. His parents had sent him to live with his aunt in a town about five hours away, and the weird part was they hadn't moved. They had only moved him. There had been no phone call, no note from a friend, and no contact to me.

But talk about an immediate answer. God must have been working on that even before I had tearfully pleaded with Him. I'll be totally truthful with you. Getting that answer from the Lord didn't feel like it helped my young heart heal faster. In fact, outside of the miraculous part of it, I felt no difference at all. But at least I had my answer, and I knew then I hadn't had to give up my future. There was still one out there waiting for me.

As a teenager, I don't ever remember making up my mind that my parents had been right in their decision. As an adult looking back, I understand it was done in love and with the best of intentions based on what they knew about the entire situation.

Even though I knew God had not set him apart as my intended future, it was a long, long time before I could let him go totally from my heart. That longing for some kind of personal closure would return to me periodically, but I knew that God had been the one who answered my prayer, and so I left it alone.

About ten years prior to this writing, I heard from him on a social website, and that led to a friendly phone call. He asked how I was doing, how many children I had, and what I was doing for a living. After I answered him, I asked him a little about his life and then asked where he and his wife lived. When he told me, I realized it was the same town the Lord had moved him to when I was just a teenager. I guess you could say that when God answers your prayer and then does something, He means for it to stay done.

That faith prayer had been my youthful lifesaving moment, and I believe it was the only way I got through that period of time in my life. When I got my answer as that young teenager, I knew God definitely had my back. Even though I felt as if I would die from the pain, I knew then that it would get better someday and that it would be right.

Praying and presenting my dilemma to the Lord had been done with full knowledge that I was ready to accept His answer, heartbroken and all. I knew that would be the only way it would work for me. It was just too bad I didn't pray that same prayer when my next love came around just three years later.

All through high school I'd been fairly successful at maintaining my Christian behavior. However, over the course of a year after my graduation, I'd become more acclimated to the worlds' version of fun, and it was then that I met my Waterloo. In the presence of this new love, my Christian values were quickly discarded, and my theory of trying to follow the rules just went out the proverbial window.

I think it's only normal for people to have a desire to orchestrate their own lives and set into motion the plans they have for achieving their dreams. But the trick is realizing that your own strength of determination and resolve will become the basis of whether you'll end up successful or not. In other words, how determined are you? If you're weak and you waver in your convictions, your goals, and your attempt to achieve, then you're left open to whoever may want to come in and run the show. It's easy to get swept away when you've not prepared for obstacles and you haven't thought out your plan of action for your life.

Of course, the Lord also has His own methods of operation and structure for achievement. One of the methods He uses with you and me is through prayer. Just as I had used His method of prayer when I was sixteen, if I had again gone to God, I would not have found myself letting go of my values and behavior quickly.

I'd tried many times to figure out what had happened inside my head when I met this new love. What had made me so inclined to just discard my own way of life and so easily throw myself into the life of someone I virtually knew nothing about? I didn't sense that I'd made a choice to disregard myself, but I had. I'd disregarded the future me. By not thinking of myself first, it showed my strength of conviction and determination hadn't been strong at all.

Because I didn't realize I hadn't thought about what I wanted in the long run, I ended up making a short-term decision that had very long-lasting effects. Nothing had come through my mind as a question mark. Nothing came to me posed as an alternative. It just happened, and I let it.

One of the things I haven't yet mentioned was that during my high school years I'd actually had two different boys in my life I thought could have ended up as part of my future.

It was my first day of high school when I spotted him. He was a sophomore. He was good-looking, and he seemed very likeable. We flirted for a long time before we actually went out on a date, and I think that was mostly because of my age. He lived on the wealthy side of town, and I was nervous about meeting his family, but when we met I realized they were not only Christians but just as nice as he was too.

When I turned fourteen, my parents allowed me to accept a date with him, but only with the promise that we double-date with my sister. That situation didn't last too long because my sister actually wasn't all that excited in sharing her date nights, but it did accomplish the task of opening up my dating eligibility.

Our relationship lasted until my family moved to another city about a year later. Our new residence was located in a very large town about three hours south of where I'd lived all my life. My heart hurt because I had to leave my childhood friends, our home church, and my first crush and recipient of puppy love. But it wasn't an option that was open to any of us, and so off we went to begin a new yet very different life.

I brought this earlier situation into my story at this time because while I was writing about the reason I might have been so available to giving myself to someone I didn't know, I began to consider a thought I'd never had.

Before I met Husband #1, I had dated two young men I believed might end up in my future. Both of these young men were basically removed from my life without any decision making on either of our parts. There'd been no breakup and no closure on either situation. So I can only wonder if that space in my heart that young girls long to fill with love made me a little more willing to throw myself toward this new person with total abandonment.

When Husband #1 came into my life, he just accepted me and took me like I belonged to him. Everything outside of my work that I thought of or did revolved around him, and it all just became okay.

During high school the guys I dated in between my first two loves weren't long-lasting, great, heartfelt, emotionally significant persons in my life. They were dates with people who were friends, and no earth-shattering relationships had resulted. There'd been no fighting and no conflicts.

Was it possible that because I hadn't had to endure ugly or confrontational situations during dating, my Christian training and obedience to parental guidelines had made my life choices too easy? Maybe I hadn't really ever tackled anything that fought back. I didn't know that I wasn't prepared like I should have been. It's truly possible that my Christian walk was never deeply challenged, and maybe I had more head knowledge about my personal convictions than I had heart knowledge.

For years I remember saying, "If only I had taken the time to pray and wait for my answer." But I hadn't, and I didn't. God could so easily have shown me whether this man was to be the husband He would have picked for me. I shouldn't have let that option flee from my grasp. I should have been more prepared and solid in my convictions about God's place in my life.

> If any of you lacks wisdom, you should ask God, who
> gives generously to all without finding fault, and it
> will be given to you.
>
> —James 1:5 NIV

Chapter

9

Mixed Signals

During one of my years in high school my older sister competed for a beauty contest, and I remember how beautiful she looked the night they crowned her as the winner. She had big brown eyes, dark features, and she was tall. One day I remember her mentioning to me that she thought it was possible her popularity in school was due to her physical looks because we certainly weren't among the popular or wealthy crowds.

Our town was basically a place where you were either wealthy or not wealthy. There was really no in between. So because of this, the school had created a rule that all female students had to wear a type of uniform during school hours. This was a huge break for those of us who were not wealthy, but I'm sure it really aggravated all the ones who were. Nevertheless, all the kids at school knew who had money and who didn't. After all, we lived in a small town.

In hair color and height I was pretty much the opposite of both my sisters, and I remember people commenting on my cuteness, which I took as being a downgraded version of my two beautiful brunette sisters. As I got older, I began to assume that my sister's statement about why people liked her must be right, and I began to take on those same thoughts. But what a disservice I did to myself! I had totally discounted me. It never dawned on me or my sister for that matter that maybe it was just because they liked us.

As that never-ending follower of my older sister, I used to watch her as she learned her lines for her parts in the school plays. While she was capable of learning not only her part but most of what the other actors were supposed to say and do, I could barely remember my address. I had always believed that her super confidence was what had fueled her love for drama and her acting ability. But years later we were sitting together and folding clothes, and right out of the blue she said, "You know I don't have any confidence. I was just acting." That was pretty typical of the method she used to clue me into certain things. But this time I just looked up at her, and I was so surprised at what she said that I almost didn't believe her. With a rather smug grin she had just admitted to me that all those years she had just been acting. When she said it with that smile on her face, I realized I had seen that same smile many, many times. It left me with a really weird feeling because I had always been jealous of her ability to lead in a group or in a play, and now I realized it had been a performance. My heart went out to her because I hadn't realized we lived in that same world. Our only difference was I wasn't able to act my way out of it.

In looking back at this, now I get it. I can see why she may have offered up that reasoning for why people liked her and dated her. All this time, all these years later I finally understand that my beautiful older sister was unsure and insecure just as I'd been.

So I'd like to voice my opinion about the breadth of my compelling line of reasoning as to why people may have included me as a friend and as a date. I want to state very loudly that living your life and placing so much importance on looks for whatever reason can be devastating when that's the only guideline you have. When you believe in your subconscious that looks are your only offering and you know you're now looking at a confusing, unsettled life, that's a tough road because looks will always fade. They're not a true guideline for who you are, who you may become, or what you have to offer. Physical attributes have their roles, but as they change—and they will—you'll begin to feel disappointed in what you see in the mirror. It won't take long for you to think that others are just as disappointed as you are when they look at you. Where then do you think self-worth has gone?

Your real beauty is not at all about your outward appearance. Yes, of course, you should want to keep yourself looking as attractive, healthy, and clean as you can, but that's not really why people will be drawn to you. What will attract them is that depth, that light that shines from within you. That's what reveals your actual beauty.

Chapter
10

Ignorance and Innocence

I graduated high school at the very young age of seventeen. The month used as the cutoff date to enter school for the next year just happened to be the month I was born. Since my birthday was only two days away from the actual cutoff date, I was always the youngest in my class. I seemed to always struggle with the more difficult classes, such as math and science. If the class had just completed the first quarter of algebra and they were ready to move on, it seemed that was just the time I had begun to figure it all out.

I applaud the kids who are super smart and can easily skip ahead throughout the school year, but sadly I was not one of them. I didn't consider it then, but now when I look back, I realize my comprehension and propensity for learning was months behind everyone else due to my age. In a kid that's huge. Since I had never considered my age as playing a part in my being a student, I also never thought that this same difference would follow me all the way into the beginning of adulthood. Graduating at seventeen and then thrusting myself forward into an adult job while living away from home wasn't something I was at all emotionally ready for.

After I had lived in a strict Christian home for so long and then gone out into the work world, freedom felt really good, but I was unaware that the ways of the secular world would creep up so easily on me. Little by little my life patterns just absorbed these new views, and small changes began to occur. I found myself not attending church, and I began going to some of the parties that acquaintances who were not fellow Christians invited me to. By the time I met Husband #1, the call of the flesh and what it offered had begun to make small cracks in my walls of Christian thinking and behavior. I was definitely not the type of person who left home and went wild, and I believe for the most part that was because I agreed with the life I had lived at home.

When I met Husband #1, I was driving around in a cute little sports car that I'd bought. My job had given my self-image a boost, and I had hope in my heart. What I didn't know was that this was a prime time for adversity to strike. You know, when you feel good about your life and yourself and it seems you've got it all under control. Somehow in that newfound strength and confidence, you become vulnerable and forget to look for an enemy who may be lurking just outside, waiting to pounce.

In thinking back, one of the things I don't remember doing was checking out my options of choices for the types of men I wanted in my life. About the only criteria I had ever thought about was that he should be a Christian, and back then if people said they believed in God, I assumed they were Christian. Oh, ignorance and innocence were not kind to me.

At home we didn't converse about much more than school, church, weekend activities, who was on the phone, or if our chores were done—you know family stuff. Life was pretty basic, and although it was quiet, it seemed normal. It was only after I entered into marriage and employment that I found out that what I knew about living life would prove to be very different from those people who were now in my life. I hadn't bothered to look for differences. I just assumed they would be the same. My parents had provided a marriage pattern of two people who stayed together and worked things through, and as very private people, they had been guarded about their personal marriage habits. In our home no one ever raised their voice to yell and scream much less use bad language. When there's ignorance of worldly values and you've been surrounded with Christian principles and friends, recognition of what to watch out for is slight. Living daily within strongly held borders of behavior doesn't lend itself to awareness of how the enemy devises his attempts to deceive.

Those many years ago when I was being raised in my family home, I don't remember the church taking the opportunity to teach the youth about spiritual warfare. They didn't explain to you that the enemy is all about deceit and being a counterfeit of Jesus. But with today's availability of teachings and programs on television and the computer, that's not at all the same story. Everything is at your fingertips. Do yourself a favor and get informed and inform your kids that there are two separate factions that will affect your life. One faction is great and mighty, and the other is ugly and dangerous.

Every day you make choices. Those choices will have something to do with either your present or your future, and every choice you make and carry out will become your past. Don't leave your home and your family ... or yourself open to whatever might be roaming around, looking for prey. Making your children aware of the enemy won't hurt them. It'll do just the opposite. It will arm them. It doesn't have to be done in a scary way, just in a teachable way. Don't let your children be innocent and ignorant of the ploys of the devil because he's very real and he is playing for keeps. Pray protection and guidance over them and yourself every day. "Be sober, be vigilant; because your adversary the devil, as a roaring lion, walketh about, seeking whom he may devour" (1 Peter 5:8 KJV).

In my life, I've found that a wise decision is to devise your own method of operation within your household and to hang on dearly to the habit of letting the Lord lead your way. Prayer, which is basically our talking with God, is at the top of that method. Have a clear plan of action and know that without seeking assistance from the Almighty, you leave yourself wide open to the ugly and the dangerous. When you so carelessly walk through life with no plan and no spiritual armor, others will choose that plan for you.

Chapter
11

Husband #1

At age nineteen, unmarried and four weeks pregnant, it was clear I had not had a plan. I hadn't really thought much about the decisions I'd been making, and now I was caught up in something I couldn't change. Your mind tries to tell you it's not real because it's such a faraway place and so much further from where you thought you'd be. I mean, how could that have happened to me? It definitely felt like it was only a dream, and my mind kept telling me if I just pretended it wasn't happening, it wouldn't be true. How could a girl with my Christian background and values have found herself at this place?

In my youth the world was so different than it is today. It's really not even remotely close. When a gal found herself pregnant and unmarried, she was immediately the topic of conversation, and everyone judged her as the bad girl. When it would happen to someone still in school, even the other girls would talk about her. The blame was always placed on the female, and the guys never had to live with the stain of bad on them. In fact, it was fairly normal for people to look at the boys as caught in the situation. There also was no questioning the subject of marriage. It was just assumed a marriage would take place, and that was for the protection of the child's birth status.

Husband #1 and I talked and made plans to get married in Nevada, and then we made the big decision to each tell our own parents. Looking back, I think that was a horrible decision for me, but that was still a decision we had made together. My mom point-blank asked me if I was pregnant, and I lied right to her face and said no. By the time we were married, I figured I'd only be about six weeks along and was desperately hoping I'd be able to play that off as an early birth. Yep, it was definitely happening, that wonderful moment with my almost husband, beginning a new pathway in my life.

This event with its hidden secrets absolutely changed my life, but knowing what I know now, I wouldn't trade it for anything. What if Husband #1 and I had never married? What would have occurred? Would I still have had my same children if I had married someone else? I don't know. I really don't. My son and daughter have both been such a great part of my life. I can't even imagine not having them, and I'm glad I don't have to find out.

I had no idea of the consequences of marrying someone known only to me on a sexual and emotional level, and that occurred because I didn't pray and wait for the Lord to answer. I just went where my feelings took me, so I'm not going to make any excuses for my behavior. But I do feel I'd like to leave you with my thoughts about common and shared values. I'd held onto my Christian standards throughout my early dating phase, and I was fortunate that the two guys I had special feelings for in high school were both Christians. Having someone in your life with at least comparable values makes it easier to maintain control. Now I did not say anything about it being easy. I just said it was easier. What I hadn't prepared myself for was that new, strong, and lustful desire mixed with an eagerness for adult life and freedom. Looking back, I realize there really had been no resistance at all, and that was very dangerous for me to put myself in that situation. God's plan for you includes being bound together or linked together or coupled together with those who share the same common values and godly standards. "Do not be yoked together with unbelievers. For what do righteousness and wickedness have in common? Or what fellowship can light have with darkness?" (2 Corinthians 6:14 NIV).

By the time we had been married for four months, I knew I was in deep trouble. I was married and pregnant. I had a big belly and a deep hole of hurt in the pit of my stomach. How had this happened? I hadn't prayed. I hadn't asked my Father in heaven if this was the person He wanted in my life. I also hadn't given myself the time to really know him as a person. My only reaction to him from the first moment I saw him was absolute want.

I had believed I was in love before, but this new emotion was something that brought an intensity I'd never felt. In looking back at it now, my guess would be it was aided by my own self, pulling away little by little from my Christian standards and conduct. I'd unknowingly withdrawn my own personal protection by not paying attention to what I knew to be right, which caused me to pull away even stronger.

My life had quickly changed, and I found myself alone most of the time. About the end of the fourth month in my pregnancy, I lost my job. Times were different then. Sexual harassment and discrimination weren't even thought of as prejudice in the workplace. In my job I'd never had a write-up. Nor had I ever received any type of warning. One morning I walked in to work and saw my replacement sitting at my desk, and it was then that I was taken into the office and told I was no longer needed. He calmly stated that I just didn't have the *look* they wanted to portray at the reception desk. I wasn't given an opportunity to work in another area I was just told I no longer had a job. At that time there were no liberation movements or policies protecting workers. Nor were there laws about those types of things. I went home and cried and cried and cried. It was an ugly time in my life, and I was embarrassed, humiliated, and so awfully hurt. It was the first time in my life that I had experienced the word *cruel*.

After my beautiful baby boy was born, I found myself absolutely in love with being a mom, and it was basically my only source for happiness. After I lost my job, and because he wasn't working, we lost our apartment. The next year or so we spent living with various relatives. By the time of the birth of my second child, my beautiful daughter, I was living alone. Our lives had been on and off, and after several years of that and after the move into my very tiny apartment, I was handed a set of divorce papers. I was scared out of my mind but thrilled at the same moment. I'd been familiar with having a great deal of time alone, but now I suddenly became acutely aware of how alone I was really about to become. But as nervous as I was and as broke as I was, at least I knew an end had come, and I knew an end always gave way to a new beginning. The sad thing was that somehow I was still in love with him and had always held out hope of change.

My son was then about twenty months old, but with a newborn, I couldn't even conceive of how I'd be able to get a job. I had no car and no money. Besides, who would watch my kids? That was a mixed-up and emotional day for me. I knew I hadn't prayed over my decisions, and because of that, my children were the ones who were going to pay the biggest price. Guilt was heavy, but the fear of the unknown was even heavier. Still there was a sensation of hope, and I pulled that toward me, hugging it with everything I had.

Several months later my mom reminded me that her sister had a brother-in-law who owned a used car dealership. I had met him only once, but by that time I was so desperate I just swallowed my fear and embarrassment and called him. I told him my situation and asked if there was any way he could help me get a car so that I could find a job. We worked out a deal for a $500 Nash Rambler, and he personally loaned me the money to pay for it. That car lasted about a year longer than my payments but by that time I had a job. That was a big reminder to me of how good God is even when we haven't taken time to consider Him.

Bringing to life this chapter wasn't an easy task because this part of my life was my initiation into adulthood. It's what set my future into motion, and it held lots of ups and downs, smiles and pain. But after I wrote the entire chapter and then proofread what was sitting right in front of me, I realized I couldn't let it go out to you the way it was. I had to rewrite and edit before I let it go.

As I went back through all the memories, I just found no need for you to see in print any of our troublesome issues or the ugliness between two people that happened so many years ago. He and I had taken two young lives and gotten in over our heads before we even knew it. You know, how do you come back from that? A part of your life that should have taken at least ten years to develop was jammed into less than three years, and brokenness was the result. I'd rather end the chapter this way with no dirty laundry hanging out and no real stories told. I've given to you what I wanted you to see as I've opened that window to my life where it all started for me and mine. But right now I'd like to take you with me into my next step of making choices without a plan, and you'll be able to see how life continued to play out for me.

Chapter
12

Husband #2

My marriage with Husband #2 took place when I was just an innocent babe of twenty-six, and believe it or not, I still didn't have a lick of sense. He was thirteen years older, and he had a secure job. Although he was divorced, he had two children that he had contact with regularly.

We met at the first meeting for Christian singles held at my church. The concept of the group was to help single men and women find Christian friends to partner up with for activities. This alleviated having to go through the constant dating ritual. It was helpful because it kept loneliness at bay and gave to everyone a much-needed social life.

My daughter was about four when I decided to move to this new little town, and going to church and joining the singles meetings provided me with that new start, for which I was desperate. I had taken a yearlong breather from any dating, and although I wanted to have a man in my life, it was really all about finding that one man who was respectable and mature and who would take care of business. Because Husband #2 was a Christian, older than me, and seemingly stable, I let my attraction to him continue instead of mentally waving him off.

Our singles group had a lot of fun that winter, heading off to go to the snow several times, and I must confess there was a lot of flirting going on within the group, which only added to the excitement. As time went on, I began to feel as if marriage with Husband #2 might be an okay fit for me. Our group stayed active, and we began to attend functions as a couple. We were still single, but we were partners in all the activities and parties. From what I'd observed during our friendship and on into our dating period, I saw Husband #2 as calm in temperament and well liked by his friends. He had the appearance of needing a home-cooked meal and seemed to be in need of some friendly support, and I attributed that to the failure of his marriage and break with his kids and household. We talked about our divorces, and on a couple of points ours were similar; however, his had lasted longer and was more family-oriented. I knew what I had been through during my marriage and divorce, and in reality, I guess I just wanted to be loved and needed, so I dug in and gave him more of me and more of my time.

One night during a discussion he asked me what my dreams and hopes were for the future. He said he already knew his and was ready to share them with me, but he wanted to know about mine. This conversation was so different for me because no man had ever asked me what my dreams were or what I hoped to accomplish. I wasn't prepared at all.

After I graduated high school, I'd gone to work and subsequently began my relationship with Husband #1. Because of my circumstances, I really hadn't taken an opportunity to look toward a goal or a dream. So when I was faced with his question, I didn't have any answer other than my desire to just be safe with my kids and be happy. He told me his dreams, and from everything he said, I realized all his aspirations revolved around local politics. I didn't know anything about political stuff, so when he began describing what he wanted to do, it sounded exciting, and I assured him I would help.

I was shocked when he presented another question to me. The question was about whether I had ever done anything illegal or anything that would make him look bad in the eyes of the press. He said if I had, that might be something that could keep him forever from his dream, so he needed my answer.

He had always appeared to be nothing other than squeaky clean, so I just froze. I didn't have a criminal past that I was worried about, but I did have something else. I began to think that if he was worried about the press finding something out, it was just possible someone might dig into my past. What I didn't want anyone to know was how I had lived my last seven years. The knowing that one of his friends or even one of the wives might find out about my being pregnant when I got married actually made me almost physically sick. I'd come to this new town to start over, and now I was faced with the possibility that if I married him, the details of how I'd had to live and how poor I'd really been terrified that part of me that was trying desperately to hide. I didn't want anyone to know about any part of it. I didn't want pity, and I certainly didn't want to encounter any more judgment. But I was so lonely and hungry for a partner. I just couldn't stomach the thought of being alone any longer. Even though I was never sure that someone wasn't going to uncover and reveal my past, I made a decision to go ahead and marry him. I was embarrassed and ashamed because I hadn't been smart about my life, and now it was available for anyone who wanted to view it. I think part of my embarrassment was based on the fact that I really inside didn't feel like that girl who acted crazy in love, got pregnant before marriage, and was then divorced before the age of twenty-three.

I had only lived in our area a very short time, so I didn't know many people, and I also didn't know any of his friends. He was doing all he could to maintain relationships with them, and I wanted to encourage that; however, I wasn't good at it. I was not only shy but now afraid of what they might see in me because I wasn't one of them.

Because I was living my Christian life again, I wasn't drinking or going to those types of parties, and any social event with me acting as hostess was held without liquor served. I was nervous around his friends, and I think they pretty much saw me as boring.

Although I had promised I would do whatever it took to help him achieve his goals, I still didn't know what that was to be. Everything involving him and a new marriage to him was scary and intimidating. That should have been a red flag for me, but instead I turned it around and began to think maybe I was the red flag for him. Maybe I wasn't a good fit for who he was.

We did get married, and in total, we were married for approximately twenty-three years. Now I know that sounds like an odd way of explaining the length of a marriage, but I say it that way because after ten years into the marriage, we separated for the first time.

We began a practice of staying apart for a year or so, and then we'd come back together for a couple of years and then separate again. We continued that practice for about ten years, and there were several reasons this type of life worked for me. It meant I didn't have to be totally alone because we had decided that if we really needed something, we would be there for each other. It also meant I didn't have to get another divorce, and I didn't have to put myself out there when it came to other men. I didn't want to date, and I really wasn't even sure I wanted a man in my life at all.

Eventually we gave in and just decided we should be roommates because it made sense financially, but after several years of that, we divorced. Enough just became enough, and although I had no desire to find someone else, he wanted a life partner. I couldn't fault him for that.

It's all about choices. Choosing wrongly in life, falling in love, and making wrong decisions is not against the law. It's not like you've committed a crime against the public, but it may become a crime against yourself. I pray you don't fall into my same trap of giving up on life. But if perhaps you already have, I want you to know there are still options and ways out. It's not giving up or having an affair, and it's not taking your life. It's not becoming addicted to drugs or alcohol or gambling. The way out is God. He's your only salvation, your only rescue and deliverer, your only true friend, and your only way through.

Being ignorant of the ugly things in life should be a wonderful thing, and I definitely believe that's what my mom and dad tried to do when they raised us. However, because that old, ugly devil can manipulate you if you let him and because you live in a sinful world, your life may turn out to be exactly the opposite of what you'd hoped for.

Life is strange. It seems the more you try on your own, the deeper you dig yourself in. It is so much easier to let the Lord guide you. Again, in looking at that situation, I was living a Christian life and prayed before my marriage decision. But I still hadn't learned to wait for as long as it takes to get God's answer. Because I hadn't trained myself in the art of waiting on the Lord, I would pray and then just go with what I felt. That is not at all waiting on the Lord.

But they that wait upon the LORD shall renew their strength; they shall mount up with wings as eagles; they shall run, and not be weary; and they shall walk and not faint.

—Isaiah 40:31 KJV

Chapter

13

Husband #3

Husband #3 caught my eye because he flirted with me, and even though I was a couple of years his senior, he made me feel young at heart. He never hinted I wasn't smart enough or that I was too messed up. He just made me feel at ease. It was as if I could be who I really was in front of him.

I know it sounds too good to be true, but there I went again, not waiting for an answer. Oh, excuse me. This time I didn't even pray, so how could I have waited for an answer? Boy, my sinful flesh really got in the way with this one. He liked me. He made me feel that I was enough, that I was wanted, and he let me know that he saw me as beautiful, inside and out. I was so needy for love and attention and he seemed perfectly capable of filling those needs.

You see, I didn't understand that I'd made plenty of those critically wrong decisions in my life because I hadn't waited for the Lord. I just hadn't put those pieces together. When I met Husband #3, I was just ready to fall for someone who gave me love and who acted as if he couldn't get enough of me. I did not think about consequences, and I didn't wonder about whether or not it would work. So I let myself fall into what I'd term as a lustful, emotional, almost nonsensical, needy love. I wanted it, and I felt I needed it, so I let myself grab at it.

During our dating we each revealed occasions of hurts and losses. His childhood was so different than mine. I found it really difficult to hold back feelings of overwhelming compassion. Boy did my sympathetic underdog gene kick in then. My imagination and compassionate qualities, however unrealistic, combined together, and I began to plan all the ways I could make life better for him and help make up for his losses.

Approximately ten months later we became husband and wife. Because we had long-term, well-paying jobs that we both liked, we decided to keep our same living arrangements for a while. That's a big lesson learned. Never put finances first in your marriage for any reason, never, not ever.

For the first six months of our marriage we lived about six hours away from each other, and because of our work schedules, we only got a chance to visit on the weekends. That was super tough for me. I'd brought this person into my life because of my needy desires for love and affection, and now we barely saw each other. For the health of our marriage I knew it was important that we be able to bond, but actually our short weekend visits were more like having a physical fling a couple of times a month. I'd spend hours making home-cooked meals and desserts to bring along so he would have a taste of home. But in reality, all of this really began to feel like we were coming together in something similar to an affair.

One morning I got a phone call from him, and he told me he had quit his job and was coming home to live with me. I was excited, but I also felt rather hesitant. Our relationship as a married couple hadn't been able to grow the way it should have, and he hadn't told me yet why he had decided to just up and quit his job. But at least he was coming home.

After we'd been together for about three months, he still hadn't been able to find work. Things had absolutely changed between us, and we'd become more like friends. We each had our own roles to play in this very nontraditional marriage. I don't believe it was ever his intention to wound me or cause injury to my heart, but sometimes when you leave out consideration of the consequences, that's exactly what happens. There were incidents in our life that caused huge changes, and eventually we grew further and further apart. At this point in my story of my marriage to Husband #3, I'm just going to end it.

As I'm sitting here and writing, I'm reminded of how I felt when I mentioned my sister's reasoning of why people may have liked her. Her conclusion was based on physical attraction and looks, but it totally left out any depth of her person. It seems as if this accounting of my marriage was similar to that because our relationship was fueled by emotional feelings and sexual attraction. We ignored opportunities to add any depth that would have kept us together in a bonded, permanent connection.

Without the Lord to help you, sometimes you mentally and even emotionally walk away from each other so far you can't find your way back.

I didn't have Jesus in my pocket at that time, and I certainly wasn't paying attention to Him. I had let go of His hand, and on my own I became lost. On my own I just couldn't find my way. But to be really honest, I wasn't sure then that I wanted to find my way. Although it certainly wasn't what I ever expected, my final marriage option became one of release. I gave him over to the Lord as His project, and I have let him go out of my heart and out of my thoughts.

Chapter
14

Husband #4

About five years after my divorce from Husband #3, I did a mental imaging of my life. At that time my job was going well, but my personal life revolved around doing chores and errands, visiting with my kids and family, and going to church. I began to wonder how really personal that was and where that would take me as I continued to go through birthday after birthday and year after year.

I still had my basic doubts about men, and I'm sure they could sense that from me, so I decided my only hope for any type of dating activity was to join a Christian online dating site. I was not at all prepared for what this brought into my life. I'd forgotten how nice it felt to have men pay attention to me, and I remember how excited I'd get before I looked to see if someone new had checked out my profile. Now I have to remind you that even though I'd been married three times and I had two children and teenage grandchildren by now, I still had that silly, naïve streak in me.

I thought when people posted their pictures on the site, these would show me how they currently looked. I also thought when they said they were active in hiking and dancing, these were indeed current hobbies, not what they used to do or what they dreamed of doing. I was confused and troubled. Trust in men had not been my strong point, and because I only wanted a Christian man, I found this endeavor exceedingly difficult to wade through.

However, because I didn't look like a good gamble for marriage based on my track record, I figured immediate anonymity was still my best bet. Signing up online would enable me to share only what I wanted to share in the beginning without lying or misrepresenting myself. I wanted to have an advantage of getting to talk to them and watch their profiles before I met them.

As time went on, I began to realize this process wasn't as easy as I had thought, not only for me but for the people who were available out there too. Before I'd signed up on the site, I just hadn't been able to find anyone who fit my criteria, although I hadn't really tried all that hard. At that time in my life I was getting really lonely, and time continued on, passing me by. I still didn't have trust or compassion for men, but my want for a partner was very strong. I would run home from work just to see if anyone had noticed me and wanted to talk, but what it ended up being to me was a relationship kind of on its own. It fulfilled me in a way that I needed. I had wanted attention and certainly a type of womanly recognition; however, after a while when I would go through long periods without finding any new hits on my profile, I would get really disappointed like it was personal. The only real thing that did for me was add fuel to the fire of knowing I apparently wasn't the right fit for any man, even men I hadn't met yet. It just never seemed to click for me. It was then that I made a decision that would cause a total change in my life. I decided it might be easier to look for someone who could become more of a companion, with benefits.

One day after I came home from work, I found someone new who had left me a message. He lived a couple of hours away, and on paper he seemed to hit many of the marks on my list for a possible marriage partner. He breathed. He loved God. He had a job, and as far as I could tell, he wasn't in prison for being a serial killer.

After several weeks of talking, we met and had dinner. He appeared to be thrilled to meet me, but I immediately wasn't sure about how to receive him because he had brought along with him two family photo albums. I was unsure how to take this because I wanted to use this first date as a way of viewing him, not his family. But he seemed nice, so I was nice and let him take me through them.

He was a very different type of person than I'd ever dated, and it was unknown to me at the time whether that would be good or bad. But I still made that decision to follow through and go on several dates with him because he seemed as if he could be a good companion. He seemed happy.

One thing I've learned about myself is that when I assessed people for dates and friendships, my decision-making process was flawed. It seemed I had an inability to move aside the heartstrings that would connect when I found someone I believed possessed the same needs and issues. Heartstrings can be dangerous because they may give off a false feeling of already having a bond with this person. I would find myself always trying to fix them or soothe them or make up for some difference. It was rather like I was willing to play nurse, and I just didn't know how to look at them and then let them go.

Many times it's those very strings that will keep you from seeing more than just the surface of people's personalities. When you wait, a deeper revelation of that inner person will unfold, and those attachments may unplug on their own.

But there was no unfolding, so I merrily went on my way and made a decision to go ahead and date him and see what occurred. After all, he seemed nice. After several months I began thinking about the possibility of marriage with him, and after I dated him for a period of time, he became Husband #4. He was actually my current husband when I met my new Christian friends.

Our life had been fine for the first year, and then overnight I found out something that caused it all to change. For the next two years it just snowballed on itself, and the differences that had begun to escalate in our lives developed into a deep wedge.

The marriage that I now knew should never have taken place was now being forced to simply lie down.

Chapter
15

Matters of Your Heart

When you are looking for a life partner, don't overlook unusual character traits and certainly don't settle. It's those types of occurrences in your life that can put dents in you, and those dents don't just go away on their own. You need to let God heal them.

Everyday life automatically brings irritations, and then on top of that, the quirks and oddities people have seem to gain in strength. Even though you try, it just becomes difficult to wade through. As time goes on, if you keep it all and don't give it up to the Lord, when those other things get added to the mix, it may make life seem intolerable.

I also truly believe that humans haven't helped themselves in their relationships because they've gotten accustomed to the word *love*. They throw it around everywhere and use it for everything. That same word is shared for feelings about your job, food, shoes, movies, chocolate, cars, television, and anything else you've grown to care about. Of course I can't prove it, but it's my opinion that the difference truly comes in when you have found someone you're in love with. This isn't just love. It's cherishing and adoring and kindly putting up with them and their quirks and putting them ahead of yourself. We want that kind of love. Being in love allows you to put very light blinders on your eyes so that you can more easily tolerate differences.

It's my thought that God has been presenting to me a view of a Christian marriage where if *both* would work at the marriage and allow God to be in the midst of their marriage, those in-love blinders could stay on. So look at the blinders you've selected. Have you picked out ones that are lightly shaded, or are they as dark as the night? I tell you it's all about your choices. Don't get ahead of God. Check yourself. Don't be responsible for moving your life in the wrong direction.

Have you ever tried to put a cooked spaghetti noodle into an eyedropper? Well, a marriage that gives you dark blinders and that doesn't have God in the middle is like that noodle. It just doesn't have what it takes to do the job. It's not the wise choice, and it's definitely not the best fit.

It was a long time after my last divorce that I learned that even at that stage in my life God could still have picked me up and set me on the path that He had chosen for me if only I'd asked Him and trusted in Him. I didn't know it wasn't too late. As a believer, I didn't know that God doesn't show prejudice against your behaviors and your mistakes. I didn't really know that God doesn't condemn you for those choices.

I'd always thought that I was beyond His help in the marriage area because I had gotten divorced. There were several Christian women who had made it a point to let me know that God couldn't bring me a Christian husband. They said that since I was divorced, God would have been going against His own laws of adultery if He brought me one. They so wholeheartedly explained that God would never go against His Word and go against His own laws. Being the insecure and totally mixed-up person as well as an expert in making wrong choices, I believed them. I was almost grief-stricken in the knowledge that I had so devastated my life that there was no option for a bright future. It sure didn't seem fair, but I just tucked that inside, wore it on my heart, and tried to hide from everyone how I felt.

"But I tell you that anyone who divorces his wife, except for sexual immorality, makes her the victim of adultery, and anyone who marries a divorced woman commits adultery" (Matthew 5:32 NIV). This scripture is an example of what was presented to me. I'm not saying it's not the truth because it is. But what I want to say is that something in their statements to me was left out. It's something I didn't understand then and they probably didn't either. God eventually gave me the realization that I needed to get on my knees and ask for forgiveness for my part in any wrongdoing in my marriages and divorces. God showed me He would grant me forgiveness, and with that forgiveness, His mercy and grace would come too.

Romans 8:1 says that if you're in Christ Jesus, there is no condemnation. There's no guilty verdict, no conviction, and no reproof. Divorce in itself is not greater than any of the other sins. However, it brings with it consequences involving a huge amount of pain and sorrow, and it produces families that live separately from each other. Divorce is definitely not in God's plan, and I'm praying you give your marriage every opportunity for change and discount the fact that divorce could be a viable choice.

What the Lord showed me was that He is willing to forgive our behavior and sinful acts based on the sacrifice of Jesus Christ on the cross. When God says He takes your forgiven sins and casts them away and they become as far as the east is from the west, that's exactly what He means. I'm a forgiven woman, and the Father allows me in my forgiven state to come before Him as His daughter with no condemnation and no judgment. It also means I can come before Him, clean and washed in the blood of the Lamb, and I can expect Him to offer to me all that He would offer to you.

I caution you in regard to the word *repentant*. Being truly repentant in your forgiveness is absolutely necessary. It means that you've not only confessed to God that you were a participant, but that you have taken responsibility for that part. It's a matter of letting Him know you don't want to do it anymore. You're saying you're determined to turn yourself around and make resolutions for change so that there won't be a repeat.

Because God is in love with you, He acts as your heavenly Father and then also acts as your Abba Father, basically your daddy God. He picks you up, dusts you off, and sets you upright without any offending manner, with no criticism, and without adding humiliation. He's always there for you. He doesn't turn His back, and it's never too late as long as you're alive.

As I've gone through these pages of marriages, I still feel there's someone who needs to know what I haven't yet explained. The opening up of my life and letting people peek inside is really awkward. You want so badly for people to not think unkind thoughts and to give you the benefit of the doubt in the brainy department. Revealing all of your personal dysfunction stories for all to see and hear is at best a prickly situation. But if one person in reading this can catch sight of a hope to grasp at and recognize they aren't alone in their confusion and their manner of trying to find love, they may take a detour in that path, which would be amazing.

When you're alone and feel as if no man wants you and you can't get it right, you may not feel normal, but you may still want the normal things. When your marriage falls apart, you have to forgo all the physical benefits that you may have had while you were married. When you're separated, it's seems worse because you're not dating, so you don't even have a close male friend or a partner to talk with or laugh with or anything. Being divorced becomes just plain ugly and usually lonely. You feel like you have stains on your heart, and you can't see your future because your vision is clouded with disappointment. Yet this pull, this unrelenting intimate and sexual tug on you never leaves. You may not want that man or really want anyone, but you want and desire the sense of that connection.

There were lots of years spent in between marriages and even quite a few spent in separation periods while I was married. When you look back at my patterns of men and marriage, you'll probably figure out that most of the time in between my relationship choices, I didn't wait for God because I had an ulterior motive. I always desired some type of relational, intimate, and/or sexual behavior. That was my deep pocket of ulterior motive. Throughout much of my life I'd tried to live within a behavior pattern that abided by as many of God's rules as I could. I did try, and I knew the basics of how the Lord felt about sexual activity without the benefit of marriage. But in truth, I didn't wait for the right one for two basic reasons. First I didn't believe there was a right man to be found. Secondly I wanted to have a semblance of normal and have that type of personal and intimate relationship with a partner. That wanting of normalcy and that desire for intimacy was driving me. It was the mental, even more than the physical that was the underlying force. That need for love and the feeling of being needed and being able to fulfill someone else is overpowering. I knew God had given humans this ability to feel pleasure in marriage and procreation. I believe that one of His intentions was that this particular bonding would continue to bring the couple back together even through daily junk and hurts.

What I want to yell out to the world is can you even believe I made the wrong choices and let go of getting answers from God because it was taking too long? I wanted to have it all. I wanted to be normal, and I did not want to indulge in the act of sexual sin. It's almost as if now, in the telling of it, like I'm someone else and I'm listening to this story and realizing this woman really needs help. But what I'm leaving out here is the fact that I didn't trust men, and I really didn't want a repeat. But I still had that horrible want for what I presumed people got from normalcy.

In my heart there had always been no real belief for myself that God could intervene because I'd made my choices in my partners, and I'd been told His hands were tied. But oh, my goodness, I was so totally wrong, and I was confused and thought I was looking for something that turned out to be not at all what I really wanted.

Don't sacrifice yourself for yourself. I was giving away me and my future for a fix I thought I wanted, and throughout the years I followed the same path with the same results. In thinking I was getting normality, I brought into my life people who just couldn't give me what I needed, and so I had to start all over again each time. It's not too hard to figure out that all those decisions, resulting in those lost years, took longer to go through and end and begin again than it would have taken if I'd prayed and waited.

If only I'd waited longer for God to reveal to me what was really waiting for me, but you see, I didn't know that yet.

Chapter

16

Loyalty at What Price?

Do you ever find yourself examining what's been going through your mind and then attempt to figure out why you're viewing and reacting to those thoughts in a particular way? Well, I have. I've done it plenty of times during these last several years. One of the issues I found and then questioned was my continuous pattern toward being loyal to whoever was my current partner. Apparently it wouldn't matter if they were treating me right or not. It was as if I had signed up and enlisted for the duty and then assumed the responsibility for making it work, whether they were trying to or not. I found myself allowing situations to continue because I didn't think I could change, and then I'd attempt to hide the issues from family and friends. What I didn't realize was that they already had perceived those issues and were waiting for me to do something about them. But knowing my own personal policies and boundaries, I still thought that I was accountable for continuing that commitment, even if my partner couldn't or wouldn't.

I was a gullible, easy-to-fool, unpretentious, and always giving person, and I've come across quite a few other women who do the same thing. My fellow bleeding hearts and I should never have been allowed out into the world alone to make selections for dates and partners.

Many times the bleeding heart will be drawn toward men who could have been listed on the graphic representation or visual aid for time bombs. Those types of time bombs have generally been fashioned and created by their being allowed to live their lives with the expectation of extra care. They may also be the dominant, overbearing, and overwhelming type.

Time bombs may offer up excuses of not having had a good start in life, or that no one has ever seen them as the good men they really are. They'll tell their sad stories as they look into your eyes and portray to you how no one really understands them all the while they're pulling on your heartstrings with their sadness and need. The super dominant ones will hold you in their arms with a powerful demeanor and sexuality. They will make you feel they not only want to take care of you but also wouldn't think of letting another man be near you.

If you took the time to open up and exam the intricate insides of these various time bombs, you'd find a bundle of characteristics. In one you may find expectations for preferential treatment, a plea for sympathy, and impartiality along with a threading of insensitivity and indifference. And in the other you may find more authoritative structure and influence, an overassertive manner, and heavy-handed dealings.

Of course, not every man with needs or personality differences or authoritative characteristics is a potential time bomb, but those who are potentials are definitely out there. They'll come into your life and look for the most comfy spot to set up camp, especially if the enemy is attempting to guide them in.

Sometimes these time bombs have lived their entire existence exhibiting themselves as the deprived and disadvantaged ones. It's possible that because of your demeanor, you wouldn't automatically assume this would be unhealthy, but wait until you're living in it. They'll have very large needs and require constant assistance, care, and support. Sometimes the pull from them is equivalent to a blood draw, leaving you feeling vulnerable and drained.

Or it may be that you have one on your hands that's very domineering and loves to rule and reign. Many times a person is drawn to these men because they take care of business, and with that, they'll have a powerful, take-charge kind of attitude. That possible deadly time bomb usually has been decorated on the outside with good looks. Their manner is appealing and allows for thoughts of having someone who will protect and take care of you.

Beware, my friend, of bombs of any type. You didn't make them, and when you decided to go out and look for dates or husbands, you didn't head directly to the bomb store. They're tucked right in with everyone else. If you suspect you have picked a potential, you can do one of two things. First you can say thank you very much and be on your way, or you can be selective and date them *only* long enough to notice the warning on their inside label. However, I would caution you if you're a bleeding heart because attachment can happen quickly for you. When you don't take God with you on your shopping trip and don't give those decisions to Him, it's probable that if you've selected a bomb, it won't be a matter of *if* it goes off. It'll be a matter of *when*.

Think about why you may be so willing to give chance, after chance to others. What in your life has happened that prompts you to gift that to them? Basically it's surrendering yourself to people who assess themselves to be more favorable or more valuable than you.

They're putting themselves first, and you're letting them do it and not holding them responsible. Of course they're going to look right at you and tell you it's not their fault if you picked them. They're just being who they are, and in truth, that's correct.

If you've been a follower all your life and you happen to partner up with that super dominant person, you won't command situations, it will be them. For sure there won't be loving talks with two minds joining and coming together. There won't be situations where you solve issues after talking them out. Generally you won't have much fun because everything that happens is done by instruction and direction or even blatantly without your knowledge or acceptance. These types of relationships won't offer to you particular choices because these partners are not usually concerned about your thoughts or feelings, and according to how you let them play the relationship game, why would they be?

I think it may have taken me several years to finally figure out why those time bombs in my life believed they had a right to act the way they did. It wasn't even something I could have conjured up. That pattern of thinking just didn't appear on my radar. It was not in my nature to automatically assume that everything revolved around me and that everything was mine for the taking either by decision or by act.

So what possesses a woman to think so little of herself? What was it within me that I gave so little care to protect myself against another person who treated me without concern or consideration? You'll find it easy to take on the assumption that the resulting problems are your own fault either because you did something wrong or because they told you that you were to blame. I wonder if on occasion it may even be that you took on an obligation to pay that price you believe you rightfully owe because you made a really unwise choice in your life. Maybe that would be a mental and emotional punishment.

When faced with the possibility that you chose a super dominant partner, you should watch him carefully during the dating portion of your relationship. That is because there are different strengths and intensities mixed into the behavior of this type of person. You won't know whether your personality can wear this type of behavior or whether this person will simply wear you.

Out of the super dominant males I've been around, most of them fully embrace the behavior of being direct, to the point, decisive, and even challenging. I think because they have a preference to lead and control, they don't consider listening to small details, and they aren't usually bent on stopping to listen. It's as if they believe they're right and there's no need for discussion or banter or giving in.

Reserved, down-to-earth, compassionate women who link themselves forever with a truly super dominant man might be viewed as committing emotional suicide. However, the same could be said if you linked yourself up to a weak, subservient, extremely needy, or passive man.

A balance of both is needed for the two to get along well. However, I think that's the sort of event that takes time, perseverance, prayer, and God's timing to answer those prayers. Find out their behaviors and moods, daily activities, temperament, and quirks, and if they've treated you as someone with value. That's why it's so important to leave out the sexual part of it. Becoming intimate will throw into the situation a completely different thought process. Stay celibate. Don't be touchy with them. Let them honor you and indicate by their behavior their respect for you as a godly woman. If the man is a godly man, he must accept God's rules on sexual behavior. If he's not godly, my word to you would be to let them go immediately.

God knows the type of person and personality you are. He knows who will be the best fit for you. Some of these types of people may not be wrong in character for others, but they're wrong if you are the same type of woman I was. I'm not here to tell you that I'm not strong in mind and that I'm not full of ideas and wants and desires, but I am here to say, "I'm a recovered passive and gullible, bleeding heart woman." I don't believe the Lord wants you to be passive. He desires you to have strength of character and morals. I also don't believe He would want you to be gullible because that leaves you susceptible to the enemy and blinds you to wisdom. The Lord has shown me how to let Him work in my life and let Him make my decisions. I've become a woman who wants a man to lead me and pray over me and look out for me and yes, even cherish me. As few as five years prior to this writing I didn't know how to distinguish between types of men. I didn't have an understanding of what was actually available for me, through Christ.

My hope is that if you're ever faced again with someone coming into your life who wants to date you but who's not a Christian, you will immediately step back. Let them know you'd be thrilled to pray for them, wish them well, smile, and move on. Please don't try to maintain a close friendship with them. It won't serve any purpose for you, and it could leave an opening for the enemy to sneak in. The Lord doesn't want you to be unequally yoked together. There has to be a combined sharing of your spiritual lives, and that can't happen if one of you isn't a true and dedicated believer.

I don't say this to you because I'm a know-it-all. I just want to give you a caution because I didn't do that and I know what comes of that. It's so easy for people to make promises about changing and going to church or believing in God. When it comes time to fulfill those promises, people may find it extremely difficult. Making a promise to go to church and become a believer isn't like saying you'll quit a habit for someone. It's a whole new life and a whole new belief, and it can't be only a knowledgeable decision. It has to come from within the heart.

Chapter

17

Damage Control?

It took me a long time to understand the Lord was teaching me that just because someone presented himself to me and said he wanted me, it didn't mean I had to accept him. God wants you to be cautious of the influence other people bring to your life. It became clear that just because a man said he knew I was the one, it didn't mean he was my right choice. It also became apparent that for too long I'd believed men when they said God had told them I was the one. Please don't just automatically assume God would tell them and not you. I personally would be very cautious of that situation. If he's the right one, God won't just tell Him. He'll also let you in on it.

Do yourself a big favor and do it the right way. Don't stumble through life and think about giving up because you don't believe it'll happen for you. Being wise and not letting your emotions get ahead of you is the way to go. Feeling guilty from bad choices and too many marriages and relationships doesn't mean you can't stop in your tracks, breathe deeply, and pray to the Lord for help. Don't think that God holds those occasions against you. He's ready at any time to forgive you. All you have to do is decide in your heart to change and then just ask Him to forgive you.

Do something you may have never done before, take the time to ask yourself what you want for your life, and open up your mind to possibilities. Ask the Lord to tell you what He wants in your relationship with Him and then ask Him to help guide you onto the path He has set out for you.

One important issue for me was that I would often think that loving a man was the ultimate. But boy has God changed my mind. I've begun to believe just loving is not enough for a picture of your future. Of course, you may think it is, and you may argue all day long and maybe never give in, so I won't try to convince you. However, I'm here to tell you that my experience has proved to me, that loving was not by itself enough.

Being crazy about that person doesn't afford you the vision to really see what the other person has inside. Love won't keep you from becoming disappointed when they show you that you can't count on them. Love also won't keep you from being torn up inside because the one you love isn't strong enough or committed enough to move into the process of giving a little and taking a little. Loving won't help you when you're constantly together with someone who doesn't care if he rubs you the wrong way. Loving won't take away the sorrow of having a person who never gives in and never says, "I'm sorry." Loving them doesn't ensure that they will love you right back. In fact, their meaning of love may be different than yours.

When that passion and first love is strong, things look good, but what happens when that fades a little bit and you find yourself married to someone you don't really know? What happens when that person in your life begins to take you for granted? You have to take the time to learn them and let them learn you. You have to pray and ask for guidance and find out what love means to them before you marry them. Blind love is just that—blind. If it's real, it'll wait until you're both done learning about each other.

New love is strong, and you're so filled with wonder that it's terribly hard for your brain to even consider these things. But it's vitally important for you to allow the Holy Spirit to stay in a position of prompting you and for God to be included in every decision.

When I found myself with someone I hadn't taken the time to learn about, I subconsciously began taking on guilt. When he began treating me in a way other than I thought he would, it became apparent that once again I'd missed it. It was tough for me to accept the fact that I'd overlooked what had been clear to others simply because I believed I loved this person. It would have been worse had I become sexually involved with him because that's an overriding, bonding emotion. I didn't think about how much blame or what I'd actually participated in, I just began to wear the guilt. Constantly wearing that shame and blame eats up self-worth and self-respect won't even show its face.

If your intended marriage partner in life is strikingly different and you look up and find total pandemonium, please don't use that opportunity to judge or evaluate just yourself. Use the opportunity to analyze your partnership and do some mental figuring to find out if this person with his quirks is someone you can not only love but also accept for sixty to eighty years of marriage. Is the person so far removed from how you live and think that somewhere down the road you'll lose your way? Does he have the same love for God, and does he have a capacity for humor and the thirst for life that you do? If he doesn't, why are you still with him?

In fact, if you're already married to a man with a totally different thought process and way of living and you're having difficulties in your marriage, you should stop, get on your knees, and go to God. Once this marriage has already happened, you really can't take it back, so try to disregard those thoughts as they come into your mind. Now this isn't the same recommendation I would make if you are being abused or assaulted. That's a completely different case, and it's one that I talk about later.

Try not to get on the treadmill of thinking, *If only.* That's a very dangerous place for a spouse to be. It causes your mind to entertain assigning blame and other options. Open up to the Lord and let Him be your wise counselor and then ask for God to help you want, to let it get better. Your first step should be asking the Lord to forgive you for any hurts you've caused to your spouse and to help you stop doing that in the future. The second step would be to go to God and tell Him you forgive your spouse for any pain he's caused you.

This is the only way in your heart to start from scratch. Forgive and then let it all go. Let the Lord have it all. You can't hold on to any of it. It's a pretty safe bet that the enemy will try to drag back every hurt and every mean thing that might have happened to you or come from you, so do yourself a big favor and don't receive these. Don't even let them look for a parking space. Whisk them away. Every time one of those thoughts or hurts comes into your mind, say *out loud*, "Get out of here, I'm not going there. Thank You, Jesus," or quote a Scripture *out loud* and then just go on with your business. Believe it or not, that could happen consistently throughout the day every day for a while. Even after you figure you've got that one knocked out, you'll find sometimes it tries to make a return visit. The amount of times these hurts come back to you is a pretty good indicator of how important it is to let them go. Why would the enemy go to such great lengths if it wasn't important for you to get this? It's with this victory you'll have freedom to think about your man and his life and your life as a couple without all the overriding emotions about failures in the past. Figure out what type of person and man he really is. Don't base it on how he's acted in situations but on how you've learned he really is inside.

Making an actual physical chart can be helpful. On the chart you can number all his good points on the left side and number all his bad points on the right side so that they're across from one another. Then go to the right side and completely mark through the bad points you may not like and you wish he didn't have, but are the ones you could live with. Then take a good look at all the good points on the left side and then go back to the remaining bad points on the right side. Now remember you've already prayed and gotten and given forgiveness, so it's time to get to the hardest part. Find a bad point that might correspond with a good point. An example of the bad might be that he is so domineering that he goes ahead and makes decisions without ever talking with you about them. A good point might be the fact that he's not a procrastinator and he never puts anything off. So you would then link the two together with a line. By the time you're done linking up the good and the bad, you'll have a better understanding of his good qualities. When you're done, hopefully there will only be a few things left on the bad side that may concern you.

If you really want to get down to business, make your own mock chart of how he may see you. Of course it won't be the same because men will always see things differently, but if you're totally honest and look at it as he might, I think it'll be quite an eye-opener.

Pray and talk with God about the bad points your husband may still have listed on that chart. Ask the Lord to help him gain vision into these areas and to become more open to changes. Remember that God is a miracle worker. Prayer for your husband without any debating, arguing, or threats toward him will open up avenues you never thought possible. After time, prayer, and some soul searching along with a change in your behavior, you may be able to *begin* a different type of conversation with him about *one* leftover item at a time. Please don't pick a time when he's watching the game or waiting for a phone call. Try to never take on issues when he first walks in the door. Let him take off his shoes and get settled into his home. Remember—he's not normally built to give you more than two or three minutes of total concentration at a time. This is not a fault in him. This is how his Creator made him. If you have a man who likes to talk, he's the exceptional case, and you, my friend, are blessed.

It was well after my children were grown when I learned it's fairly easy to change a child's behavior with positive reinforcement. There's no reason to think it wouldn't have the same beneficial rewards when utilized on an adult. Instead of saying, "I hate that you never spend any time with me alone," try saying something like, "You know, I was just thinking today how great it is that I have a husband who comes home to me every night. Thanks, babe." Well, you know what I mean. Can you see the correlation? At some point in time, because men like to be built up, he may even quit doing some of the things he used to do without you. You know, it might not hurt you to change your ways and volunteer to do one or two things you wouldn't normally do just to be with him. Try thinking of his habits and his comings and goings. Is there something he enjoys doing that you could find yourself liking or learning to like?

I realize you may be thinking, *Why is it I'm always the one who has to change?* I've heard that so often from women, and I've even said that in the past. My only response to that is that apparently you have the ability to throw down logic and maintain understanding.

Therefore, God allows you to be more moldable and pliable. To change, that's exactly what's needed. If you treat your husband with respect as God instructs you to, whether he deserves it or not, he'll see you differently. It may not take away all the ugly stuff, but that coupled with prayer will definitely have an impact on him. If you would just let yourself wink at him or give out a big smile when he does something in the house, even if it was his so-called job, that's huge. It actually doesn't hurt, and it goes a long way toward him thinking that you think he's a big deal. If you love him and you want to keep him around, that's a surefire way to get started on it. If he did that to you, wouldn't you be more likely to feel loved, which might result in you feeling sexier and more playful? It might make all the difference in the world.

Everyone has his or her quirks, and everyone has good and bad points. First Peter 3:1–6 speaks about women having a submissive spirit toward their husbands. It talks about that offering to them, an ability to see their wives in purity and reverence of their inner beauty. Showing him respect and being in that submissive spirit then offers to you the possibility of winning him over based upon your behavior. The Scripture says that's possible without you having to open your mouth and speak words.

Be the woman who tries. Be honorable to your position as a wife. Try not to let yourself be afraid that he will take advantage of the situation. Pray first, and if you do what the Lord expects you to do and it still doesn't work, then at least you know you've done everything you could. Let the Lord guide you from there.

We've talked about submission and the power of it, and if you've decided to be that respectful woman of God, it will go a long way toward helping in your day-to-day situations. Your man might calm down a little himself and see that you're not weak nor are you attempting to take over. You're just trying to be the loving partner by submitting to his prayerful leadership.

In the realm of eternity, your life isn't even a tiny wisp, but in thinking about living your full life on earth, it seems like a long time. I don't want that time, whatever time it may be, to be devoured by someone who sits on my dreams, my goals, my ministries, and my love. I never again want to get left behind. I never want to feel as if I've been run over and left for dead. I also don't want to be with someone who needs to get more out of the relationship than I do. If you're single and all wrapped up with someone who doesn't share your dreams and goals or at least care enough to help you, it's too easy to lose sight of who you are as your own person. If you're not careful, you'll actually become incapable of letting yourself dream at all, and that eventually becomes too dangerous emotionally for you and too disappointing.

You may have gone through marriage after marriage after marriage after marriage like I did. But remember the bad choices. They're like that proverbial bad penny. If you don't do something in your life to change the situation, they'll show up again. When I say change, I mean you need to look for the real solution, which is God. God can heal the past and the baggage that we carry from situation to situation. In His healing, He offers us hope and true power and authority to go forward with newness. I don't have to be gullible or vulnerable with God making those decisions for me. I just have to learn to pray and wait for an answer, no matter how long it takes. I need to remember that my track record proves I personally don't make good life choices, so I need to put God in control and let Him show me which choices are the best for me. Trust Him to do that. Place your loyalty in Him. He's the real deal. He's the one who deserves it.

To be totally honest with you, sometimes it takes a little while, and sometimes it takes a long time to get God's answer. If you know that in the end God will pick out for you the very best choice and you won't have to redo life, isn't it worth the wait?

Chapter
18

Failure's Not an Option

When I came home and saw Husband #4 packing the moving van to leave our home and begin somewhere else, I had really mixed emotions. The part of me that wanted peace and harmony and freedom from strife was happy. It was the other part of me that was panicked. Watching him, I knew in my heart this was my last marriage, and now it was over. There wasn't going to be another marriage of any type for me. In that declaration to myself, failure hit me right in the face. I sat down and looked around and told myself that it was true. I had failed in every one of them, and I had failed in recouping what was left of me. Somehow my private life had become a total failure. How was it possible to crawl my way out? But I absolutely had no intention of trying again because I knew it would turn out exactly the same way. I remember thinking, *You can't do this again because your picker's broken.* Yep, it was true. My picker was broken.

I didn't know people were capable of just one day deciding to treat you as though you meant nothing to them. But if you're unfortunate enough for that to happen to you, be very careful how you speak and think about yourself. You can convince yourself through your words to be whatever you say. There were lots of times when I didn't pay attention to what came out of my mouth. I didn't take time to realize those ideas swirling around in my head telling me I was a failure as a wife, did just as much damage as they would if they'd been spoken out verbally by someone else. Telling yourself all day long that you're ugly and fat and unworthy and not lovely and not loveable can only bring despair. Words can never be taken back, and those spoken words stay in the atmosphere forever. Instead, tell yourself you're beautiful inside and out, lovely, and worthy of God's love. Even if at the time you don't feel that way, say it until you do believe it. People every day and in all kinds of situations speak and think so harshly about themselves, and I was once one of them. Emotional anguish and feelings of unworthiness had been sowed into my life. It basically left me unable to sort out what had been occurring and why I was constantly making bad choices that affected not only me but my children as well. However, the Lord has graciously taught me that feelings of not being worthy don't come from Him.

When you don't take the initiative to protect yourself from a person who may want to enter your life as someone who's too dominant or too weak or who's a user, you leave yourself wide open to conflict. For the entire time you're with them, you'll be forced to struggle or lie down. The problem is really simple. It's like being sentenced to an emotional prison. Even if you do make it out, you more often than not have many emotional cuts and bruises and, yes, even some scars. I pray you won't allow yourself to join that cell block.

Living my teenage years in a home with structured borders and guidelines had not prepared me for someone who had totally opposite behaviors and ways of thinking. If perchance you find yourself in this same situation and you haven't yet made that choice to marry, you still have three basic options. Although these options aren't what I would call wonderful, one of them still affords you a chance of recovering before the actual rescue is needed. You could back out totally, or you could continue in it and conform to the other person. Or you could try to stay in it and hope and fight for change.

Your first choice of backing out totally would leave you brokenhearted. The end result would be more beneficial. The pain would eventually go, and you could still have a future.

The second choice of continuing and conforming means living with a husband who believes he always knows best. In his mind he is right, and you need only to conform. It's possible the dominant one will never give in to anything and will have a condescending attitude. The user will probably attempt manipulation, work you via annoyance, and badger you in everyday situations. Either way you won't be in control. You'll be living your life through him.

Of course, the third option of staying and fighting means probably living in a hostile environment day after day. The atmosphere of the home would likely be unsympathetic, unreceptive, and patronizing. After all, it's a battle.

If you're a softer type of woman and your partner is super dominant, he not only doesn't want you to win but also doesn't want to lose. It's his belief he's okay just the way he is. If you constantly battle, you'll soon develop the "I just don't care anymore" attitude.

The good choice to make is to not step out of your realm of knowing, and don't venture into someone else's unknown territory of living. Existing in situations that you know are not right or you feel are against your beliefs will weigh heavily on your spirit and undoubtedly bring distress and regret into your life. One thing I didn't find out about until much later was that sometimes partners try to make the other one feel guilty. If they can make you guilty of something, even if it's not true, they believe that releases them from their guilt. You've just become the new guilty person, and it's as if they've become exonerated. I had to have help with that one because I would never have figured that one out by myself. When I tell you I was innocent in thought, I really mean it. That type of corrupt thinking had never played in my head. I had no spiritual armor, no known way to fight or even to know what to fight against.

I'd been taught in church and at home that upon marriage the man assumes the role as head of the house, not the boss but the leader of the two. Because I had not heard my mom verbally disagree with my dad, I assumed that if a husband told you something as the leader, he was giving you the right way to go. However, that may only work when both are Christians and prayerfully attempting their relationship.

As a believer, with all the humans on earth, don't you know that without a plan and constant spiritual surveying of your life, the cheaters, liars, consistent manipulators, and overwhelming tyrants will just appear? Take the time to sit down one day and do a review of someone else's relationship and you'll see how easy it is to pick out who leads and who follows. You'll find it just as easy to see who will stand out as the one with the stronger will of the two. Watch the followers as they get confused about their partners' behavior when the partner begins to act differently or badly. This may cause the follower to take on the guilt and believe they are at fault. They may think that some failure in them caused the action. As the viewer, it's strange when you witness the actions of the people behaving badly and observe that there's no indication of guilt. You'll notice it's almost an automatic reaction for the follower to jump in and act as if they should take responsibility of fault. It's almost like they're at fault by default.

Those are the types of things that people hide from their friends and family because no one wants to be humiliated. When you're intimidated easily, shy, and naïve, it's easy for you to become embarrassed. I had carried my values throughout high school, and I had given over my boyfriend to the Lord when my parents told me to end it. Then after all that, just three short years later I walked headfirst into a relationship with someone who couldn't have been more wrong for me.

There are people who'll think of me as an exceptionally unwise person and someone who doesn't even deserve a real chance. Believe me, there were many times when I felt that same way and would have agreed with them. But during this last five years the Lord has shown me why I took on all those different pathways. Of course, I want you to know that God didn't set up any of those wrong choices, but when He designed man, His design included our ability to freely choose.

I made those choices, but it was never God's intention for me to walk another path. He had always intended for me to go down the one path He had devised specifically for me. It was God who brought into my life these new Christian friends who became the beginning of my walk into safety and truth. Through my friend's words and advice, I somehow became willing to at least try to listen for God and then wait for His instruction.

God was able to open my eyes to the reasons I had taken the direction I'd gone. He didn't give up on me, and somehow He never let me quit. Very slowly He revealed the gaps and voids in my life, and since that time He has been busy filling them up with Him. Hope has become a new but solid word in my life. I can't adequately express the importance of staying on the path that God sets before you, praying about all your life's decisions, and waiting before you make them. Don't let your short-term emotions and feelings determine your long-term future.

Chapter
19

Building That Confidence

What was it inside of me that left me so willing and available to give myself away to someone just because he said he wanted me? Why had I tried so hard to make someone else happy and not myself? Why hadn't I seen worth in me?

The Lord has answered a lot of these questions, and He's taken page after page of my life and set it before me. He was giving me the opportunity to understand where I went wrong and what it was that would have convinced me to make the decisions I made. He caused me to view and then contemplate my why.

One afternoon I got into a discussion with a friend from high school. The talk was primarily about divorce and the affect it had on our lives. He said that during the years after his divorce he had continued to have unresolved issues with his ex-wife. He became determined to make a final decision about one of those issues, and he knew some of his friends wouldn't think it was a good one. When he told me what it was, I asked him why he'd come up with that particular solution. I knew there were other avenues open to him, but he felt this would be best. He said he loved himself too much to make any other decision.

When he said that, I felt as if that was the most remarkable statement I'd ever heard. I remember asking him if he was kidding me when he said he loved himself, and he said that he wasn't. I was actually dumbfounded, and to be honest, I was really unsure whether I believed him. First I'd never actually heard anyone say that about themselves, and secondly I would never have thought a man would ever be capable of expressing something so heartfelt. So I talked with him about it for a long time and came to the conclusion that he absolutely did have that love and that he had also placed a worth and a value on himself. I had never in my entire life thought about loving myself. I don't know why. I really don't. But it's rather unsettling to think that something that important was never a yes or a no, it just was never a thought at all.

Mark 12:31 says Jesus commands you to love your neighbor as yourself. I knew that I'd not only heard this Scripture but read it in the Bible many times. I had always tried to be compassionate and treat people with care, so I think I just pulled my normal trick. You know, letting it slide right past me and not really giving it any thought because no big red flags were waving. I'm not sure my ears had stayed tuned in long enough to even pick up on the words that said we were to love them as ourselves. Right now as I look back and think about my decisions and my lack of confidence and personal value, I don't suppose I even liked myself much less had love for myself.

That people-pleaser portion of my personality was possibly the creator of my need to always defend someone or to offer them chance after chance. But that never gave me an opening to think of me. I always deferred to the other person. It's as if somehow the other person was more important than I was, and I felt I had to plead their case. Even as a child I would let other kids have their way to keep the peace and sometimes just to be nice. I was always that person rooting for the underdog, which meant no one, including me, thought of me in a way that would make me the primary and not the secondary.

It was always so important to me that I knew people liked me. When you have no self-esteem or self-value of your own, if someone doesn't like you, then it's as if no one likes you. Sitting here and writing these chapters of my life, I realize that the Lord has done such an amazing unearthing of my past. He's done it with such grace and mercy, never leaving me feeling stupid or sad or sorrowful or questioning. That was only me. From the moment I left high school and then certainly after I met Husband #1, I began living a life I was unprepared for and unschooled about. I was inexperienced in many social ways, and I was in way over my head in that outside world. I began to give little thought to what I was doing or where I was going and just began living for the moment. I went to work, but during the rest of the time my focus was on my new love and whatever he was doing. I found I gave little thought to my family, my upbringing, my beliefs, and my love for God. Now don't get me wrong. I know we all have short periods of time when we're just enjoying life and couldn't care less, but this became an everyday thing for me. I wasn't going to church, and I was letting other people influence me. It was completely the opposite of how I'd lived the majority of my early life.

When you're living against what you feel in your gut is right, that kind of existence eventually births a battle inside of you. Your wrong behavior continually nags at you, and you just aren't able to get peace. You know what you're doing is wrong, and the comments and looks from your family let's you know of their disapproval. I had absolutely been living in a way that I was not only unprepared for but one that I didn't believe in my heart I should have been living. I basically felt like a traitor to myself. If you're truly living that opposing life, there will come a point when you have to make a decision. Even if you try to keep putting it off, not making a decision eventually becomes a decision. An example of this is like voting for politicians. In real-life politics when someone comes up for reelection, if you don't vote at all, that is like a vote for the incumbent or the person who presently holds the job, because you made no choice of change.

Because of the physical problem I'd had while I was growing up, I always walked around with an internal cloud of shame hanging over me. So when this new love, this future Husband #1 entered my life, not knowing any of my previous problems, it was finally my chance to be accepted and loved for who I was, or so I thought. I didn't have a good opinion of myself, so I don't think I was ever comfortable in my own skin.

Many people assume ignorance is stupidity, but it's really not. It's being unaware of something and having a lack of learning about it. So I may have been unlearned in certain areas, but I was not stupid. I'm done holding myself responsible for that first unwise choice of bringing someone extremely different into my life. I'm also done holding myself responsible for not loving myself. You can only make corrections and alterations when you have the knowledge and understanding for valid life choices.

Confidence is the major key to success, and it's necessary when discouragement comes. Without it, you'll find yourself insecure in decisions, and remembering your mistakes only encourages you to shy away from exposing yourself to the possibility of making other wrong choices. Confidence is imperative if you want to start your spiritual growth and education into God's character. It begins with taking your lack of self-confidence and inability to believe in yourself and pulling that all in the forefront. Bring it out into the open. Don't hide it and don't ignore it.

The first step on the confidence ladder has to be to rebuild from the ground up, and God is especially good with rebuilding. He's the best general contractor known to man. To build that personal worth and belief means allowing yourself to be opened up to a total examination and then staring right into the vulnerable parts of your life.

The first place most women will begin their search is on the outside. But your personal worth can't have anything to do with your physical looks or body because that's the part of you that changes and shows wear and tear and age. The enemy loves it when you don't focus on your internal problems but stay focused on insecurities about your weight and your outward appearance. Ladies, let's face it. Some women are just physically more attractive. They always have been, and they always will be. Do you want to place your value on a thing you can't ever change? I hope your answer is no. Your value or worth has to come from your inside beauty, so work from the inside to the outside instead of the other way around. Please don't be so focused on what's previously occurred in your life that you'll be unable to see the beauty that God sees within you.

Remember when God forgives you of anything, it's over and done and gone. He totally forgets it. Do you? Hanging on to that old stuff is like putting a barrier in the pathway of your future and hanging a U-turn sign on it. Letting those thoughts remain dominant in your heart will never allow you to recognize your significance. The images of your yesterday with times of hurt, shame, conflict, scandal, and possible embarrassment will cloud everything else. It won't even allow others to see you differently if that's how you continue to present yourself.

Upon recognition of what God's opened up to you, ask Him to remove the hurt as well as the vividness of what happened and ask forgiveness and give forgiveness. Learn to recognize the Lord's voice. Pay attention to the Holy Spirit and what He says, and He'll keep you on the straight path. Praise Him under pressure and worship Him in the midst of criticism. That will keep you strong in the storms of life. Be confident in knowing that the Lord is there to bring you through. You can believe that He loves you without conditions. He will never forsake His love for you, even though you will disappoint Him and at times ignore Him. Keep that knowledge that God loves you without strings, forever and always.

Believe completely in the fact that God loves you more than anyone ever could and will never love you more or love you less based on anything you've done or haven't done. Believe that if no one else existed in the entire world, Jesus would still have died for you. Tell yourself you are no one's captive and you're not fearful because you have Christ inside of you. This continuation of speaking faith allows your value and beauty within to become a true reality in your life. Say it every day you live on earth, and it will eventually shine through your face and into your actions. Your real worth is more than outward appearance, and the real you shines through when you believe in how much God loves you and how much worth He's placed on you. Go ahead and act just like you know your God-given potential.

I hope I've been able to convey to you that God can be trusted. Take your troubles as well as feelings of lack and unworthiness and mentally place the whole bundle right in front of God. When you give that to Him and He relieves you of those burdens, you gain a knowing inside of you that gives off a confidence of His love for you and your value to Him. When you trust in Him enough to give Him everything, you will see that He will never turn you down because you're precious to Him. You may try to take the burdens back by worrying. If you do, pick them all up again and hand them right back to Him because He's still there waiting with arms wide open. He'll never punish you or shame you for your giving and taking issue. He just continues to be there for you because He's your number-one fan. He's on your side.

Chapter

20

Trappings

After I was married and divorced from Husband #1, even though I was still very young and healthy, my dating life never got back into any type of rhythm. Of course I was working, and time was limited. But the men just didn't seem to respond the same way to me. I was the mother of two children, and I knew that eliminated some men, which was fine with me, but what else was up?

Of course my approach was all over the place. I wondered what was wrong with me. Was it because they felt I was damaged goods? Maybe I wasn't pretty enough, or maybe it was all about that five extra pounds I carried after I had babies. Or maybe my personality was the culprit because they saw me as needy and they could sense that. I'd also heard that some men have issues with women who've had babies because it caused them to see women in a different way. Who knows? Well, I certainly didn't, and although I had no real desire to get married, I did at least want to have a date with a nice guy now and then.

Wasn't our needing someone what we were supposed to expect? Wasn't that how it had been designed by God? Five years before I wrote this, my new Christian friend had told me that someday I'd find out how much Jesus loved me and I wouldn't need the love of a man. At that time I had no concept, not even a clue of what that meant to me or to my life. I absolutely didn't have any picture of clarity or truth of that statement. I'd grown up thinking that when you were ready to settle down, you needed the other half and that your spouse would then complete you and that you would complete him. Didn't that have to be the way it was? Could you go it alone and be happy and fulfilled? Whenever my mind would go back to what my new friend had said, I immediately felt as if I was being told I had to have less than I wanted. Would God expect me now to live alone in celibacy because I'd made the choices that resulted in divorce? I didn't want to live alone. I'd always desired to have someone to act as my marriage partner and lover. I hadn't grown up thinking about college and a career. I'd grown up thinking about being part of a normal marriage and being crazy in love. What was that dream now? I didn't know if there really was anything that was called normal, and if there was, what was it because it sure wasn't anything I'd ever had?

For quite a long time my mind consistently went back and forth, reflecting on my friend's statement. I knew it must be something really important for me to figure out because of how long it had stayed with me.

I'm the type that likes to investigate and figure things out. If there's something that just stays in my mind and I can't put it all together, it just won't leave me alone. Because of my longing to be loved, I felt sad in thinking this part of my life just might not happen. Was I never going to get what I thought everyone else had? After all, I'd made my choices, I'd been divorced four times. My turn was done, and it was over. I think I just believed my friend was letting me know I was supposed to give up and let it go. Maybe he was telling me to be brave, be good, and love God, and God would make that be enough.

I know I'm making it sound kind of pitiful, but that's what I thought back then. Even people close to me said the Lord couldn't bring to me a godly husband because I was divorced. My heart wept over that thought. How could God hold it against me when my wrong choices had started so young in life?

It was quite a while before I began to grab onto the little pieces of wisdom about God's desires for us, especially in regard to His mercy, grace, and forgiveness. The Lord was very methodical in how He presented all these bits and pieces to me. He knows me, and He knows you. He alone knows what it will take to bring you truth that you'll completely accept from Him. Someday those tiny glimpses would come and show themselves to be truth, but for that time in my life they were still just glimpses.

I had always thought that God had given us other humans for fulfillment in the area of love. I guess I had been separating my love options—a husband down here and God up there. I thought the way it worked was that I would bring to the partnership my good attributes and talents, and my other half would bring to the table his good attributes and talents. I was hopeful that together we could make one whole person. What I didn't know then was that if you have a love relationship with the Lord, you should put Him first, trust in Him, and rely on Him. Then you have a permanently bonded connection. He uses that connection to begin to fill those voids and lacking areas of your life with Him. But I'm getting ahead of the game. Although I was beginning to learn what it was I was supposed to understand, I didn't actually learn that lesson for quite a while.

So my new Christian friend's statement would every now and then continue to pop up in my mind. I would think and pray about all the possibilities, study and make my notes, and write down all the potential ideas concerning what my friend had said. But again it was a long time before I figured any of that out—all those things God had spoken to me, all those pieces I was trying to put together.

Because I was spending so much time with the Bible and thinking and looking for revelation on this particular subject, I also learned a lot about the Lord. There was also a better understanding about what my new friend meant when he told me about finding out how much Jesus loved me. You may be sitting there and thinking, *Oh, my goodness, this gal is really dense. Why hasn't she figured it out yet?* But remember—my way of thinking about love was separated into human love and God love. I still had no way of figuring it out because in my mind I was thinking that even if I loved the Lord so much my heart could burst, I'd still need a man. Oh, I was so stubborn about the ideas that rolled around in my head. It was as if once they were there, they stayed, and the door out was being held shut. But eventually a tiny little crack allowed a new thought to penetrate my mind. One day a speck of hope came. Just maybe the Lord had something for me I didn't know about.

I had lived a long time and believed that because I'd made my choices, they were a part of a past that couldn't be changed. I knew God was in the business of delivering people, but up to that point, I hadn't really understood that He was in the business of delivering *everyone*, which had to include me.

I want to remind you I'd been a Christian for a really long time and had tried to live my life the best I was able. I wasn't always successful, and I had periods when I would ignore God because I wanted to do my own thing. I always kept coming back and trying again. I had recommitted my life to Christ several times, but other than that, my Christian walk hadn't moved out of the realm of just trying to follow the rules, loving God, having faith for others, and prayer. It seemed as if my life was keeping me in a state of disrepair, and I found it difficult to manage everything that was on my plate. Emotionally I was a wreck, much because I had so recently gone through my fourth divorce. I hoped that no one really knew what was going on within me, and it seemed like life was doing its best to wear me down. Somewhere deep inside me I made a conscious decision to hang on and do the best I could. The problem was that my faith and trust in the Lord always included other people. I still had not put myself down as the primary subject. Was this one of the reasons I hadn't found a love for my own self?

I know now that your walk with Him is never over and that you'll discover new things through Him constantly. You'll continue to walk and learn and walk and learn until you get to heaven. But back then, although I was willingly to pray and believe for others, I guess I just couldn't put myself in a mental place on the altar and understand that God wanted to heal my past. My life wasn't an accident. I'd walked my own way, determined to do it the only way I knew how. My self, had never presented myself, with understanding that my life, with all the ugly, all the hurts and all the disappointments, could be moved into the realm of a past, but a past without the pain.

There was a speck of hope, that wonder of the possibility that the Lord could absolutely love me enough to keep me from always feeling the loss and need in my life. That speck, just as my new friend had said, gave me just enough desire to take that first step. I still didn't know how anything like that could happen, but I allowed that little piece of hope to take me further.

Encountering difficulty in your life can result in pain and long-lasting issues, and you can carry that bundle around for a long time. Each time you add to the pain and stuff it in that bundle, it gets packed in tighter, and it's heavy. When violated areas remain in your life for long durations, they become common to you, and it's natural for you to make allowances for them. They become a package, you and they. Wherever you go, they go.

Whether it be abuse, neglect, molestation, divorce, or some other devastating occurrence, it's fairly normal to blame yourself for circumstances and take on guilt. There may be times when you don't feel you're responsible for blame, but you still played some type of part. Eventually that part, in its self, will begin to nag at your subconscious and cause frustration, and sooner or later guilt is birthed.

There've been times I've let circumstances get the better of me, and even though I knew I wasn't responsible, I still assumed liability because the guilty one hadn't. It was an age-old issue. When no one stepped up to the problem, I usually appeared.

When you find yourself heavy into fault and self-reproach, you might believe yourself to be unworthy or not clever enough to deal with options and decisions. Or it could be you've had a partner who continually blamed you, making you appear stupid in front of others if you didn't display the fault. Speculating and being fixated on why you do what you do will almost certainly bring some form of culpability to yourself. It's like a no-win situation. Even if you weren't to blame for the original decision, you'll find some blame somewhere, and then you'll group it into that bundle. Once it's in the bundle, you sling it over your back, and you walk around with it.

When I see a guilty person passing themselves off as innocent and purposely laying the blame on someone else, that really gets to me. These people will drill it in so harshly that the innocent ones begin to believe what's being said about them. These victims who've dealt with these patterns for extended lengths of time find themselves living with an enormous degree of remorse. If you don't access God for help then, things can become very ugly in your life. Letting the sadness, darkness, and unworthiness dwell within you could depress you, and you then become a prime target based on your vulnerability. In my opinion this is when you should be screaming for help, but often while you're going through it, it just begins to look as if nothing's ever going to be different. It's too deep, and you're too tired of trying.

I know in my adult life I continually hid my feelings, and the only strong emotions that did pop out were anger and frustration. When you let the enemy take you into depression and darkness, you don't think clearly, and feelings of being unloved and unwanted and not necessary will come easily. When you're in trouble, disillusioned, and just plain worn out, it's very easy to talk yourself into believing that God understands your suffering and will therefore let you slide and not hold you accountable. It's much like how I handled my tucking-in and hiding. I thought if I just didn't think about it, it just wouldn't be. So I understand where you're coming from. I've been there. But that's not how it works.

That person who doesn't reach out to God in that intimate, personal way could just take their own life because they want so badly to escape their pain and distress. But what they don't understand is that without God, there is no real help.

Think it through and truly grasp the fact that as eternal beings, when earthly life is ended, that's when your real spiritual life begins its eternity. After your physical death your spirit continues to live on forever in heaven or in hell. So whether you feel so violated you want to die or so wounded you'd rather just dig a hole and fall into it, neither one of those is the answer. Reaching out to God, pleading for His help, and pouring your heart out to Him is your only answer. Be wise, stop, and pray. Remember these choices will determine your future.

Removing God and giving up and making that decision to end your own life could bring you to a judgment of *eternity*.

Anguish, torment, suffering, agony, torture, and despair are only some of the human words used to explain what man may experience in hell.

So please, please remember that it's not over until it's over. Give God a chance to solve this for you. Remember He designed your path. He knows how to get you back on it.

Chapter
21

Battlefield of the Mind/Pit

My frame was not hidden from you when I was made
in the secret place, when I was woven together in
the depths of the earth. Your eyes saw my unformed
body; all the days ordained for me were written in
your book before one of them came to be.

—Psalm 139:15–16 NIV

You are an eternal, spiritual being individually formed by God,
and as a human, you've been given a physical body with a soul and
a spirit. Your soul is basically comprised of your mind, your will,
your emotions, and your particular personality. It's the part of you
that God designed to make you unique from any other. It's also the
part of you that lends itself to what is called the flesh or the sinful
nature of man. This is where your soul is drawn to the non-spiritual
indulgences of life, including sexual activity and desires outside of
marriage. But your spirit is eternal, and because God made you in
His image, His spirit and your spirit have a connection. "Then God
said, 'Let us make mankind in our image, in our likeness, so that

they may rule over the fish in the sea and the birds in the sky, over the livestock and all the wild animals, and over all the creatures that move along the ground'" (Genesis 1:26 NIV).

The soul with that carnal nature is your challenger. You will find it craves the opposite of what the spirit knows to be the best route for your God-chosen path. Unless you allow the Holy Spirit to lead your mind in its thinking, your mind will be guided by your flesh. If you're a believer and you've welcomed Jesus into your life as your Savior and Redeemer, then the Holy Spirit is residing within you and is there to help guide you.

As a Christian, satan is your enemy and your contender, and the sinful surroundings of the world are your battlefield. Bombardments of temptations, negative thoughts, guilt, accusations, shame, worldly imaginations, and multitudes of other desires and pleasures come before you constantly.

While in heaven, the enemy held an extremely high-level position, but he was found by God to have iniquity in him because he believed himself to be worthy enough to be as God. In the end one-third of all the angels chose to continue their allegiance with satan, and as a result, they were all cast out of heaven. The enemy's reign of terror is due to his vile hatred.

Because they've fallen but have not yet been sentenced to their eternal judgment, they have the ability to carry out spiritual warfare. Scripture speaks of them as the spiritual forces of evil, but they're more commonly known as demons or evil spirits. They have the ability to carry out this warfare or what's typically called their demonic activity twenty-four hours a day. This spiritual battle is centered on you but takes place between the demonic evil forces and the heavenly forces. (See Daniel 10:12–13.)

One of the enemy's best methods of destruction is to prompt you with thoughts and guide you toward actions. He insinuates that the Lord is either too busy for you, that He just doesn't want to be there for you, or that it's too late for you. He is absolutely devoted in his attempt to make you feel as if God won't fulfill all the promises He's given to you.

When God created man and woman, it's my belief the Lord knew there had to be powerful distinctions between the two genders. From the very beginning man was formed to be physically stronger and had a greater muscular structure. I believe He prepared the man for an intensity that would carry him through wars and pain and utilize his logical point of view, allowing him to provide protection and defense without regard for his own life.

God made woman to physically bear and carry the children. Some women speak of a love that begins with their child when they imagine their belly getting bigger and having thoughts of wearing maternity clothes. These happenings may occur even before she feels the baby move. This female woman that God made has been gifted with a capacity to nurture and love. Though she may be emotional, she was created as the softer side of the two genders.

God structured the family unit to really only work with these two specific sides. This first side is the more determined logical thinker and protector, and the second is the more emotional, nurturing, and trusting side. In my estimation a woman begins life as a trusting female human being, believing for the good until it may become the death of her.

I've been around women who learned to pretend as if their lives and circumstances are okay. I know this because I was one of those women. Many of them have internal screams that come out verbally sounding like excuses or attempts to pacify someone in a given situation. When you continually respond to questions about why you're acting a certain way and you give back excuses, those are normally voiced so that no one will really know what's going on inside. But those excuses are typically screams inside your head and heart, and they are really cries for help. You don't want someone to actually hear the screams because then they have to be dealt with by someone. Overwhelming waves of emotion will cause you to believe there's no way out, and you understand that once that scream is voiced, it's too late. Now they know.

I can still hear the tone of voice of someone close to me saying, "You shouldn't be so depressed. It'll be fine." People also said, "Oh, what you need is a boyfriend. That always helps." My ears heard so many people say random things that were just common fixes for any old ailment, but the words had no value and no solution or promise. It didn't matter how many times I ignored them and told myself it wasn't going to be better. There was no fix, and it wasn't going to change, I still secretly hoped somehow it could. The more that people tried to get me to listen to them, the deeper I dug.

Those words that come from your mind and then out through your mouth easily trap you. The enemy loves waiting for you to destroy yourself, especially with your very own words. Saying, "I am the way I am, and I can't change. I've tried," or saying, "Nothing good ever happens to me," only births depression, defeat, hopelessness, and failure. Speaking negative words about having diseases, addictions, and fears only brings life and breadth to despondency, vulnerability, deficiency, and powerlessness.

You might as well have hired a thug to come in and beat you up, leave you for dead, and let you lie in your own pain. The enemy has no real truth in him, so when you react to his promptings and then follow them, it's you who have inflicted your own suffering. If you continue to speak damaging and destructive words out of your own mouth it ends up working you, against your own self. Soon you'll begin to see yourself as crippled emotionally and maybe even physically. Remember—the tongue has the power of life and death in it. "The tongue has the power of life and death, and those who love it will eat its fruit" (Proverbs 18:21 NIV).

Somewhere in the middle of learning and allowing God to delve into the deep part of my past, my personal atmosphere was heavy with memories and a heightened sense of awareness. There were a couple of times when I got a visual in my mind's eye of how the enemy worked in my life and why he had been so successful.

In this visual the enemy reminded me of the cowboy in an old cigarette advertisement. He was dressed in jeans with a cowboy hat on his head, slouching over a shovel. He had a cigarette hanging out of his mouth. His hat covered his face in a shadow, but I could tell he was wearing dark shades. I knew immediately that shovel was the tool the enemy used.

I kept wondering why my mental image of the enemy included a cigarette, and then one day I got it. I'd simply forgotten how many years I had struggled to quit smoking. One day I told the Lord I'd made up my mind that I was never again going to voluntarily smoke another cigarette. Somehow God absolutely honored that statement of determined faith, and my physical and emotional cravings just ended. It was as if in my personal and unwavering decision to quit, He simply did it for me.

There were several times after that when I had thoughts of smoking, but it was never what I would call a craving. Still every once in a while even when no one was around, I could smell it, and there were times when I'd have dreams of someone forcing me to smoke. So when I think about this mental picture, which included the cigarette, I know he's reminding me that it's not over yet, that he's not done. It's a true reality of how cruel he is. I haven't smoked for more than seventeen years, and yet here he is, with that token temptation hanging out of his mouth. So don't underestimate the sneaky one. He's definitely your enemy, and your face is on that target.

Occasionally there will come times when I get up in the morning and I know for some reason it's just going to be one of those days when I'll feel melancholy. You have no joy, but there's no real sorrow, no laughter, but you're not crying either. It's times like that when you should have your spiritual ears up and your spiritual nose to the ground, smelling for the enemy. When you're not on top of your game and you're not girded with your spiritual armor, it's easier for your mind to wander. Mine usually heads toward my memories, which guides me directly into my past. It's strange because you never get lost going there. It's as if your subconscious sneakily grabs out at you and pulls you into a moment. The odd thing is that during these times I'm generally not drawn into thinking of pleasant memories. I go directly into the ones that caused pain. That, my friend, is a giveaway moment. That's when you know the enemy is on patrol.

When I thought about the mental picture of the enemy and when I realized the shovel was a tool he used, I knew he'd be standing right at the corner of Memory Lane and Past. When you travel down that long road to a memory that hasn't been resolved and is still without forgiveness, and still holds deep pain, it's easy to take that turn into your past. You immediately begin reliving the experience, the hurt, the shame, and the embarrassment that began your course of devastation in the first place.

When the enemy meets you on that corner, he offers up that shovel to you. When you let go and dwell on feelings of being tricked, offended, swindled, and misled, that's when you've just taken that shovel and are unconsciously digging into your own pit. You know the enemy has to be laughing because he doesn't even have to dig. You volunteered to do all the dirty work yourself. It gets a little bit deeper and darker each time you visit. Eventually this memory pit with all that heaviness of emotion becomes so deep you can't walk out. And you silently scream and scream, but nobody really hears you.

Pain and the losses sustained and the inability to walk up into the light all represent failure for you. Once again you couldn't do it on your own. You weren't able to get past this. Each try left you with those same memories and no release and with a sense of weakness. When you have willingly allowed those feelings and resulting emotions to continue to come to you and you accept them, you're actually creating your own destiny.

When you permit the enemy to have power over your thinking, you become vulnerable, and depression, oppression, intimidation, emptiness, and hopelessness easily travel right into your soul. Don't let him choose your reactions. Each time you allow him that alternative, you're being nudged deeper and deeper into a pit of turmoil, unrest, and self-rejection. Honestly I believe he will take you as far down as you'll let him, and he doesn't let go on his own. The enemy is in battle. He doesn't just step back. He came seeking to overcome and devour. Part of his plan is to not let you see yourself as God sees you. He wants you to constantly look at your life through the darkness so that you don't see the truth and the light. He just wants you to react, not think.

I'm not sure if you'll understand what I'm saying or if you'll question it all. It's possible that a lot of people believe this type of discussion about the evils of a fallen angel called the devil is a bunch of nonsense. They'll believe that all the talk about his method of operation and dark glasses and pits of wounds is just made-up noise. I realize that to them the ideas of something they can't see having that much pull and influence in their lives would make all of this too religious, too out of proportion, and too spooky.

I have no option but to do my best to explain that there really are two factions in life around which everything revolves. One is good, and one is bad. You won't see the spiritual war, but it's raging. God's angels are fighting for you, and the devil's fallen angels are doing battle against them. If you believe in God's Word, you can read it for yourself. "For our struggle is not against flesh and blood, but against the rulers, against the authorities, against the powers of this dark world and against the spiritual forces of evil in the heavenly realms" (Ephesians 6:12 NIV).

It's crucial for you to understand that spiritual warfare occurs twenty-four hours a day every day, whether you choose to believe it or not. Hiding your head and not looking up doesn't change anything and doesn't make it any less real. There is a devil, and he does travel in the darkness of ignorance and falsehood.

Because warfare goes on with or without your acknowledgment, wouldn't it be better to be a victor than a victim? The memories about your past and the ugliness sowed into your life attempt to present themselves to you much like sadness. Only you know how many times you've tried to stop thinking about it, but it still comes back. That's because this is a spiritual battle not person to person. God wants you to be free, but the enemy never wants you to be released into peace.

When you try to do this without God, every advantage you might believe you've gained is really only temporary. You can tell yourself all day long to just quit thinking about what you've been through, but it only takes something as simple as a song or a smell to bring it right back. You will never on your own resolve the damage and pain. It'll always accompany the memory. You will never be able to fill that deep emptiness where trust and hope should be because this battle is spiritual. It doesn't get solved by will or determination or wishing. It's not that you've failed. It's because you can't do it. This is not in the realm of what you can humanly do. But God can, and He wants to. Asking and then allowing the Lord to take the offending rubbish out of your past and replace it with love, understanding, and peace is what will let you move forward. Don't wait. Don't contemplate it. Your solutions haven't worked, so let the Lord heal you. My prayer for you is that after you read this, you'll be convinced that if the Lord would do it for me with my years of insecurities and my four failed marriages, He can certainly do it for you.

> Cast your cares on the Lord and he will sustain you;
> he will never let the righteous be shaken.
> —Psalm 55:22 NIV

Chapter

22

The Truth about Warfare

Now the serpent was more crafty than any of the wild animals the LORD God had made. He said to the woman, "Did God really say, 'You must not eat from any tree in the garden'?"

The woman said to the serpent, "We may eat fruit from the trees in the garden, but God did say, 'You must not eat fruit from the tree that is in the middle of the garden, and you must not touch it, or you will die.'"

"You will not surely die," the serpent said to the woman. "For God knows that when you eat from it your eyes will be opened, and you will be like God, knowing good and evil." When the woman saw that the fruit of the tree was good for food and pleasing to the eye, and also desirable for gaining wisdom, she took some and ate it. She also gave some to her husband, who was with her, and he ate it.

—Genesis 3:1–6 NIV

In the garden of Eden, the enemy, who was disguised as a serpent, enticed Eve by using an inhabitant of the very garden in which she lived. The serpent was apparently familiar to her, and she'd probably seen it many times. It was also entirely likely that the serpent routinely talked because when it talked to her that day, she was not fearful or even surprised. All in all, Eve was obviously comfortable in the garden with all its inhabitants, and it was there that the enemy presented to her the test.

I've read the beginning of Genesis many times, but I had always missed a really important part of satan's initial testing. The temptation he offered up to Eve that day was verbally packaged as a question, but it had a lie tucked into it. When satan asked Eve if God had told her not to eat from any tree, I always missed the word *any*. She offers back her complete statement indicating God had only told them not to eat of *one* tree, the tree in the middle of the garden. I don't know, but I believe Eve really missed on this one. She should have realized something new was happening when he began to question her specific directions from God. I doubt she'd ever been given any reason to question God's motives, so why this time? All kinds of alarm bells should have been going off, but none did. Maybe it was because of her comfort level, or maybe it was because the serpent had eaten other fruit with her while she sat amongst the beauty of the garden. Or maybe it was because he arranged his question to almost sound as if it was the beginning of a gossip session. *God really said that?* We'll never know the answer to that while we're on earth, and who knows if any of us would have acted differently under those same circumstances?

The whole scenario in Genesis 3 about the fall of all mankind is contained in four paragraphs, and within the first sentence it tells you the serpent was craftier than the other wild animals. I think that point was justly proved.

I don't believe Eve picked up consciously on the word *any*, but I do believe it may have prompted her subconscious to start her on a path of listening. The devil had taken a woman who was totally comfortable and happy and had so easily manipulated her by slipping in a carefully thought-out question. Eve would have no real idea of the extent of her choice.

I can't personally envision Eve as an unintelligent female because she'd been formed by God, and as the first woman on earth, she (along with Adam) was one of the first models for the human being. But I doubt Eve had ever had to make a choice about anything of significance during her entire life. There was no sin or shame or skepticism in the garden, and she was able to walk around freely, naked and not ashamed. They walked and talked with God. Their life was perfect. Eve had always been able to have anything she wanted, and she had no reason to expect trickery.

The enemy, much like a soldier in the military, knew that before he attacked, he had to secure his ground first, and he did that by weaving the word *any* into his very first sentence to Eve. Because she didn't call him out on it and end the conversation, he knew that he could move to the second part of the temptation and that would be the actual attack, the part that hooked her.

Eve should have chosen loyalty, commitment, and faithfulness to God, but she didn't. Instead she went for the visual appeal of the fruit and the presentation of desire for gaining wisdom. At that moment she opened herself up to the idea of wanting more. These same types of enemy maneuvers happen all the time in everyday life. You're presented with options for behavior, desire, and even with sexual opportunities. Sometimes you make the right decision, and sometimes you don't. "No temptation has overtaken you except what is common to mankind. And God is faithful; he will not let you be tempted beyond what you can bear. But when you are tempted, he will also provide a way out so that you can endure it" (1 Corinthians 10:13 NIV).

One of the examples I give of a temptation combined with a choice, is one that involves dating. As a Christian woman, you have an understanding that God has set out biblical parameters regarding behavior between two unmarried people. In an effort to stay within those biblical guidelines, you've decided to make a rule that you're determined to keep. You've realized the biggest problem that might occur is intimacy, so in order for you to bring the least amount of temptation to yourself, you decide to utilize a taxi in going to and from your dates. Your plan involves him not being alone in your car with you and you not being alone in his car with him.

So you've had a couple of dates with one particular guy and your rule has been working fine. You really like him, and you're excited because he seems really nice and very attentive. This particular night you're having a wonderful time as the date progresses, and then he takes your hand, looks you straight in the face, and asks if you would forgo the taxi just this one time. He asks if you'll allow him to drive you home because he has something important he'd like to talk with you about. Immediately your heart beats faster, and you feel new emotions and thoughts coming into your mind. Because you feel comfortable with him and you want to find out what he's talking about, you decide to just this once waive your rule and go with him.

Now if you're a woman and reading this, you already know how many different scenarios could come about as a result of your decision to suspend your own rule and walk out alone with him and get into his car. With that choice, nothing might happen, and he may just want to be alone with you when he tells you that he cares for you and wants your relationship to become exclusive. Or he may want to give you a gift, and he may think giving it to you alone would be more romantic. Or he may want to profess his love to you, and in doing so, you both may begin to move toward being more intimate with each other. But another option for this might be that someone is reading about your disappearance this very next morning.

You don't know. You won't know the end until it happens. Will it be too late for you? Will it be that you've only broken your own rule, or will it be that you find yourself now involved sexually with someone? Or will it be the end, when they find your body? I know that really sounds drastic, but these things happen. Prayer over your decisions is a necessity. It's also essential for your protection because things and people are not always as they appear. Eve didn't see the devil in that snake suit. She saw a comfortable friend. When she saw the apple, it appeared to be a luscious yet simple fruit, and Scripture says it was pleasing to her eye. But look where it took her.

God asks you to follow His path and His rules for a reason, and that's because He knows the end before it happens. One temptation, one prompting of the enemy, one deceptive wavering of the truth, one eye-appealing deliciousness, and only one decision is needed to yield to something that may change your life and take your future away.

Don't live your life without including God. Always stop to pray. If a person involved tells you that you don't have time to pray about it, my advice would be to step back and not take any action, until you have prayed. It requires such little time to say, "Lord, help me. I don't know which way to go." It doesn't have to be lengthy. God knows your thoughts and your heart. He was ready before you opened your mouth to ask for help. But always wait for His answer. Remember—He's the only one who knows the future.

The Lord says He uses our times of trial to grow us and develop our perseverance, and perseverance brings to us maturity and completeness. Give God the availability of being God and working it out as He sees best. Remember He knows the end. Of course, that won't stop the enemy from sneaking around in a shroud of doubt or skepticism, causing you to question where God is in your situation. When you encounter doubts and questions about why things aren't moving along like you think they should, you need to remember that you don't have to entertain those thoughts. Get a clear vision of what you prayed for and then put forward your faith to believe and trust in your Lord. "But when you ask, you must believe and not doubt, because the one who doubts is like a wave of the sea, blown and tossed by the wind. That person should not expect to receive anything from the Lord. Such a person is double-minded and unstable in all they do" (James 1:6–8 NIV).

Don't give up on what you know in your heart to be spiritually true and remember who's in control, and by the way, that's supposed to be God. Peace is your signal. Peace is a sign that means you have given it over to the Lord and you're standing in the knowledge that He'll take care of getting you an answer. Peace brings freedom and allows you to find that right direction without frustration or indecision. God's got you covered, and He loves you enough to bring the very best result for you.

Spiritual strength and courage are absolutely necessary when involved in spiritual warfare. In Ephesians 6:10–20, you'll find a full description of your spiritual armor of God and its intended purpose. Be on your guard, take your position, and be strong in the Lord and in His mighty power, putting on the full armor so you can take your stand firmly against the devil's schemes. The fight isn't against our human enemies. It's against principalities, the powers, the world rulers of darkness, and hosts of wickedness.

Putting into perspective God's explanation of our spiritual warfare, I imagine the devil and his fallen angels are similar to our army. Because of the enormity of the numbers of them, they're probably able to cover vast amounts of territory. I've read fictional stories about this, and I think I agree with their summation. It makes a lot of sense to me that these fallen angels may be territorial and continue their post in a particular area for the time they have left before judgment. It's like being on an assignment. That would be the perfect way for them to know every person in your bloodline and to watch them and manipulate them and listen to them. They have watched your ancestors all the way to the present generation for their weaknesses and failures and probably their successes as well.

Of course the devil has only one-third of the angels, and God has the other two-thirds. With that, I definitely don't want to leave out the absolute power of God, Jesus Christ, and the Holy Spirit.

I truly believe what makes the enemy such a counterfeit is that he wants people to think he's as powerful as God. But he's not omnipresent and therefore not able to be everywhere all at one time, and he's not all-knowing, so he doesn't know your future or God's complete path for you. He only knows the past, he absolutely does not know the future, except what has been spoken by God and given in the Word.

Although the enemy does have real power, it's landlocked, if you want it to be. It's like he's closed in and blocked from using power against you because the only advantage he ever has over the believer is the one you give him. If he tries to pull something over on you, go to your Abba Father, your daddy God, and tell on him. Of course God already knows, but He wants you to work it out by asking Him to help. God is your protector and defender against any and all, but He wants you to choose, to ask Him.

Now when you have an issue that you've handed over to the Lord, don't let worry get to you because worry doesn't have the potency you may think it does. It's not tangible or definite. It's fictional and made by speculation. It's just another tool the enemy can drop at your feet, hoping you pick it up. Worry can't change anything. It's of no value to you. When you worry, it's as if you're telling the Lord you don't trust Him.

Please don't let yourself always question God and His purposes. Never, never, ever, give up your expectation of the miraculous, and don't quit. Be firm in your faith and in your trust for God and let Him battle for you and let Him work His miracles as He will. "And we know that in all things God works for the good of those who love him, who have been called according to his purpose" (Romans 8:28 NIV).

Tell God often that you trust Him, that you know He's good, and that you believe He loves you. Be secure in the knowledge that He'll bring all things together to work for the good. If your end result is different than you thought it would be, recognize God is the one who made you and knows you inside and out. Be aware He's the one who set out a specific plan for you and is the one who brings it all together. He knows how it ends.

When you're out in the world and have not given your life to Christ, the enemy doesn't really need to get in your way too often. But once you've become a believer, your spiritual battles really begin. The world and all it has to offer continually brings compromise and options of behavior before you. In reading your Bible, you'll find that God has already given you directions on how to be strong in spirit and has provided teaching from His Word about the authority you have through Christ. Of course you could just let your life be whatever the enemy wants it to be. You could live your life with no victory, no healings, and no joy because that might be presumed as easier. But would it really? Would living an unfulfilled, dominated, and possibly crippled life be easier?

Being prepared for battle is not for wimps. You have a helmet of salvation and a breastplate of righteousness, and your feet are fitted with the readiness that comes from the gospel of peace. You have the belt of truth buckled around your waist, and you are wielding the sword of the spirit, which is the Word of God. You hold the shield of faith while you pray and take your stand in defense against the evil one.

Ephesians 6:16 says your shield of faith extinguishes *all* the flaming arrows of the evil one. It doesn't say *some* of the arrows. It says *all*. But that's only if you actually use it. Your shield has to be built on strong, firm, and enduring faith to act as your protection. Earthly shields are built to protect you only physically, but the shield of your spiritual armor is built by perseverance through trials and determination. In the building of your faith, that shield will become mighty, and the endurance makes it capable of protecting your spiritual life, even in the onslaught of physical attacks, such as diseases or sickness.

In Isaiah 52:12, it says the Lord will be your rear guard as well as your leader. In simple everyday terms, it's my belief that particular Scripture passage means God's got your back. He's covering you, and He's there in defense of opposition. Now of course these battles aren't fought physically, they're spiritual battles fought with your defensive spiritual weapons. God has already faithfully equipped you with those, and through His Word, He's trained you. For you to be effective in battle, you have to be attuned to God's leading, and when you speak, speak the words that He gives you, the very words of God. His words are truth, and if possible, use specific

Scriptures to battle your particular issue. "What we have received is not the spirit of the world, but the Spirit who is from God, so that we may understand what God has freely given us" (1 Corinthians 2:12 NIV).

In the fight you must use what He's equipped you with. Your weapons are your absolute belief in God and your trust in who He is, and in knowing what He's said and standing firm in faith. Along with that your restraint of negativity and questioning is vital. Be powerful, be big in God, stand firm, and don't waver.

"Be alert and of sober mind. Your enemy the devil prowls around like a roaring lion looking for someone to devour. Resist him, standing firm in the faith, because you know that the family of believers throughout the world is undergoing the same kind of sufferings" (1 Peter 5:8–9 NIV).

In this last Scripture it says the devil *prowls* around *like* a *roaring lion.* You know what that means? It means he's showing himself to be a counterfeit. It means he lays in wait in the dark, creeping around and stalking you, pretending to be this ferocious roaring lion.

When I began checking into why the lion is listed as the king of beasts, I found that it's basically because the lion has strength and regal beauty. It's very powerful and roars loudly with courage and boldness. Well, the enemy used to have beauty and strength and a royal bearing, but now he can only *act* like he's a lion. He doesn't roar boldly. The first time you hear about him on earth, he's clothed as something else and deviously misrepresenting himself.

You'll find through your spiritual travels that the enemy is a counterfeit in many ways. He takes God's good and copies it to be the opposite. God intends for you to have health, and the enemy intends for you to have sickness and be useless. The devil knows the past, and he knows the Word, so he knows his ultimate fate. Now that Jesus has taken your place on the cross and given Himself as the ultimate and perfect sacrifice, the enemy can't win. But he still wants to rob you of your authority, your joy, your health, your finances, your family, and your peace of mind.

In relationships he'll step in and provide that smooth-talking, good-looking bad boy for you so that you won't want to wait for the man of God's choice. He's also well aware of what you want because you voice it all the time. He works hard to make it happen with the wrong people and the wrong circumstances by enticing you.

Don't underestimate him. The army of evil spirits is lurking around and trying to trick you. The damage is caused when *you* allow him entry into your thoughts or actions. If you let him reign in your life and don't give God the honor of being first, then God hasn't let you down, you've let yourself down.

Adam and Eve gave up their authority over the earth when they opted to believe what satan presented over what God had said to them. When he suited up in that serpent body, he tricked Eve into questioning God's position in their lives and His true intentions toward them. When Christ gave His body and His life as your sacrifice on that cross, He was able to regain all of that authority that God had given them. Before He left to go back to heaven, He gave you back that same power and authority to be used through Him in His name.

Stay strong, get big in faith, trust God, and rely only on Him. Don't listen to negative people or negative thoughts. Do not let them be that counterfeit. Don't listen to the spiritual enemy's call when he tries to tell you that you're not worthy because that's an absolute lie. God has a love for you that's so strong, nothing you could ever do would change His love for you. So keep your eyes only on your

Lord. Stay powered up with the Word of God because stamina is a large part of the faith stance.

Remember it's not about works. It's about how you believe. If you believe correctly and hang in there with Jesus, the rest will be brought back in line.

Chapter
23

Promptings and Companionship

Genesis 2:18, 21–23, reveals that the LORD God said it wasn't good for the man to be alone and therefore He would make a suitable helper for him. After causing the man to fall into a deep sleep He took one the man's ribs out of his body. Then the LORD God made a woman from the rib He had taken and brought her to the man. The man said she was now bone of his bones and flesh of his flesh and he called her *woman* for she was taken out of him.

As this woman, you're designed to be the helpmate of your husband and to stay by his side, helping him accomplish his objectives and strengthen his direction. By nature, it's very possible that God gifted to you an extra dose of persuasion and feminine influence to help you in your task.

I've always been interested in the differences between the minds of men and women. I know God had a purpose when He designed women with their distinctive qualities and the men with characteristics all their own. But I have to be honest. I've often wanted to question why God would choose to do it the way He did.

Women often take issue with men's lack of listening to their wives. I've been to marriage seminars and listened to ministers on the television, and I've picked up quite a bit of good information. But the best piece of information I've ever personally heard came from a regular man. He said he was aware that women were able to carry their to-do lists in their heads; however, for the most part men weren't built that way. He stated that while men actually did listen, they heard only specific details, which they then tucked into a compartment in their brains. His term for this behavior was compartmentalizing.

Now that's quite different from women because women will normally react upon what they hear and see through their feelings and emotions. While the man normally doesn't experience that emotion when he hears something, the situation comes to him more like a fact would.

I don't really understand a lot of it, but it helps me recognize that in their natural makeup they don't hear the way you do and they won't react the way you do.

So one of my many questions is this: Does the man ever really catch what you're throwing out? If I answered my own question, I'd say, "I personally believe that would be rare based on what I've learned and witnessed." So ladies, let's not be too hard on them. They're not really wrong. They're just different, very, very different.

Listen for the Holy Spirit's prompting in this regard. One of the enemy's strategies is to get you to listen to him because he wants you to react to his emotional taunting. That's exactly what Eve did when the enemy presented her with the apple. She listened to him. But if you listen to the Holy Spirit, He'll guide you into keeping the enemy from getting in the middle of you and your logical husband or intended partner.

The enemy offered to Eve an opportunity for greater wisdom and a bite into some very juicy, pleasing to the eye, sumptuous fruit. If you listen to the enemy, you've just allowed yourself to be manipulated, and the resulting destructive thinking and actions will affect not only you but your home atmosphere and your family members as well.

In my honest opinion the woman in the marriage has a much more profound part to play within her home and to the members of her home. It's my belief that there is an intensity built into the female. Some might refer to it as an influence or power of womanly persuasion. It's your ability to be perceptive and discerning that will aid you as a helpmate. These emotions and attributes, all of which were given to you by God, also enable you to utilize that sensitive, emotional side for listening for promptings and hearing what the Holy Spirit has to say. As a believer, every part of your life will forever be a choice for either what's right and within God's character or what's wrong and what leads to the carnal, sinful nature.

One of the examples I like to use involves the sport of fishing. Imagine the enemy standing at the edge of a lake, wearing fishing gear, holding a fishing pole in his hand. On the line is a lure and a big hook, but you can't really see the hook because it's totally covered with bait. He's done that so the fish won't have any idea about what's going to happen, but he knows it's an eye-catching tidbit to the fish. He knows you (the fish) will be attracted to the lure, and of course, the attached bait looks very enticing. He then casts out the covered-up hook and waits to see if you bite, and when you do, he reels you in. You won't realize what happened until it is too late. The enemy pulls this trick so often and does it so well that if you're not listening to the Holy Spirit's promptings, you won't even recognize the enemy as the fisherman. You may just be going about your daily routine. One minute you're in a good mood, and the next you feel depressed and sad. Now you're starting to replay in your mind some things that have recently happened that hurt your feelings. There's no rhyme or reason for it, and at that point you don't really challenge it. Later when your mood develops into temper flare-ups and you begin to lose your patience, if you haven't by then realized you're in a spiritual attack, you'll assume it's just you.

That's exactly what the enemy wants you to think. He wants you to take that blame because that brings you into another level of guilt, and wondering what's going on. You may begin to question yourself, and you won't even realize that you really didn't do anything to bring this on, except *not* stop the enemy.

Had you listened to the Holy Spirit, He would have been able to tell you to be at your ready. He would be the one whispering into your ears to have your spiritual eyes open for that hidden hook.

Now that situation doesn't sound like such a horrible ordeal, but with this, the enemy was just testing the water. He was laying his groundwork. He's got a temptation ready for you, and he wants to make sure you'll take the bait, so he's luring you into a mind-set of being disgruntled, depressed, and maybe even sad and disappointed. It's much easier for him to get you to take the bait when you feel lousy. Staying in your personal walk with the Lord, talking to Him, and receiving from Him is the easiest way to safeguard your victory. When you do this, the enemy's attempts at attack just have a greater chance to fizzle out. "The weapons we fight with are not the weapons of the world. On the contrary, they have divine power to demolish strongholds. We demolish arguments and every pretension that sets itself up against the knowledge of God, and we take captive every thought to make it obedient to Christ" (2 Corinthians 10:4–5 NIV).

The enemy is clever in his willful distribution of mean, ugly, and perverted thoughts that will randomly come to you. He and his fallen angels have been around longer than you, and they've watched the people within your generations. They know the addictions and perversions that have plagued your bloodlines. They listen to you talk, and they have witnessed your actions. The enemy definitely has an evil spiritual influence in what is presented to you, and the power of suggestion certainly can bring anything you've done or said out loud back to your ear and back into your thoughts.

When the enemy comes, it's in the hopes you'll think everything that happens is incidental or circumstantial. But as a follower of the straight and godly course, you need to be painfully aware of his devices and his pretentious and deceptive ways. "Finally, brothers and sisters, whatever is true, whatever is noble, whatever is right, whatever is pure, whatever is lovely, whatever is admirable − if anything is excellent or praiseworthy − think about such things" (Philippians 4:8 NIV).

Keeping your mind filled with the Lord and His goodness and with pure and admirable thoughts helps to keep the enemy at bay. Reacting to bad moods and bad attitudes and listening to and spreading gossip are just offerings of the evil one. Holding grudges and not forgiving are also his offerings to you. Remember—satan's job is to prompt you to follow him, but your job is to resist that prompting and only react to the Holy Spirit. Proverbs 4:23-25 speaks about guarding your heart because everything you do flows from it. The passage reminds us to keep corrupt talk far away from our lips and to keep our eyes looking straight ahead.

Your walk with the Lord is faith-based, and He's already placed within you the measure of faith and His authority. He doesn't move on your behalf because you get emotional and cry and act sad or go into hysteria and moan and behave pitifully. He wants you to recognize that He has given you charge over your own self, and He wants you to be victorious. Get *big* in the Lord. Don't let the enemy bully you. The end of the Bible, written by authors inspired by God, says the believers win! In God's realm it's already done. These skirmishes are used for your strength and growth, not for you to weaken, give in, and become drained and feeble.

Your God, who looks at you through the blood of Jesus, sees you as perfect and righteous through Christ's blood. You're His child, His creation, and He loves you with an unconditional love. He sees no ugliness in you, and you'll never have to feel unworthy before Him. No matter what you've done or what's been done to you, God's love for you never changes. He doesn't love you more because you're good, and He doesn't love you less because you act badly or make wrong choices. He just loves you because He *is* love.

Please don't compare God to any earthly dad because no man on earth can live up to God's standards, principles, and values. And it may be that you didn't have a good dad, but you can believe and depend on this one. He's true and trustworthy. He is painfully patient and knows that if He can get you to understand who He really is, what He can do, and just how much He really loves you, you'll be unstoppable. Let the Lord be your Master. Don't walk around in agony and despair, and don't fail to recognize that your life is eternal. The largest portion of your existence will be spent in either heaven or hell. If you choose God, you have life. If you don't choose God, the only other option after the world is gone or after you die is that other place—the dark, foul-smelling, fiery, worm-eating but not destroying your body place. The place of eternal torment, the place God made for the devil and his bad angels. But if you don't choose

God, it's the only place left to go, and it will be forever. There are only those two options. Choose *life!*

If you feel broken and bent, there is a way to get well again. I've lived it. Jesus, who was born into flesh, knows what you're about. When Christ was on that cross, He took on all of the hurts, offenses, deception, loneliness, despair, sins, iniquities, mental anguish, and wounds of the body along with other things we don't even know about. He had all of that on Him when He died. He wanted to take it all, everything, leaving nothing behind.

That in itself gives you options, options for healing, restoration, hope, and standing on God's Word for His promises. The ultimate sacrifice of Jesus' body and His blood paid the price for all forever. You only need to choose Him. As a believer, when God looks on you, He sees Jesus, the perfect sacrifice. He sees you through the blood of Christ.

You can count on the Lord always because He is always there, and there will never be a moment when He's not present. There will never be a time when He is unaware of your every thought and need. There is never going to be a second when He looks at you, shrugs His shoulders, and walks away. He said He will never leave you or forsake you, and that's it. That's all. He said it, and it's true.

> Be strong and courageous. Do not be afraid or terrified
> because of them, for the LORD your God goes with
> you; He will never leave you nor forsake you.
> —Deuteronomy 31:6 NIV

Chapter
24

What God Can Be to You

From the very beginning God has allowed people to make choices based on their own free will. Choices—that's what all this is about, not just for me or you but for everyone. The options we have available and the decisions we make from those options will determine our futures. Please try not to freely toss them away. Use them to bring God closer to your life. You can walk around with dents, with a lack of what you need, and with voids where there should be fulfilled life, or you can let God bring to you everything He wants for you.

Earlier I mentioned that my new Christian friend had tried and tried to explain to me about God's love for me. He told me very simply that I did not have to consider myself as alone and single because God could fill that role of being my husband. My mind totally disconnected on that one, and I knew I had no conception of what my new friend was telling me. I'd heard other people mention that same thing, but I didn't believe them. It wasn't that I thought they were lying. It was just that same old recording in my head, and they were just moving their mouths. I know that sounds really tacky, but for you to understand what I mean, I need you to let me tell you the straight story, the one that comes directly out of my own life.

I had listened to them, and while they were talking, my brain was telling me it was a proclamation made by people who had been married for hundreds of years to the same person. I believed their statement had no authority in its reasoning. How could they know that God could act as my husband? How did they suppose God would be able to quench the physical and romantic desires I longed to have fulfilled? I wanted to know just how God as my Creator, Redeemer, and Comforter could be my hand-holding partner? How could they make that statement without ever having been in my place and probably without ever having this need in their own lives?

I just couldn't get my head wrapped around it. I'd spent my entire adult life looking for that type of love and that type of husband. So yes, that thought was as foreign to me as the initial one was when my new friend said that someday I would find I didn't need the love of a man. I guess in reality I have to admit I was just mixed up in my head and totally confused about my fixation with love and what I'd hoped it would bring.

Somewhere in the back of my mind I sensed there must be something to this inference that God could be my husband, but it still held no logic. I just didn't know. I was totally unprepared, so I stuffed it away for later in much the same way as I did with all the other things I didn't understand about God.

At that particular time in my life I no longer had any idea about what a relationship between husband and wife was supposed to be. After four divorces I'd learned very little about the concept of a godly marriage. I actually came away believing that most marriages that looked good on the outside were just ugliness wrapped up in pretense. I felt as though I had enough information in the study of differences of marriage partners to get a college degree, and yet somehow I had failed to ever pass my classes.

When talking about God being a husband to me, my new Christian friend had stated that along with that, I would be able to enjoy having an intimate relationship with Him. Honestly that sounded very odd, but I knew my friend well enough to give him a little latitude with that and decided I'd just wait and watch and learn. Little by little I began to open my mind to the idea of what might actually be involved in God taking on the role of my husband. I'd begun to identify several of God's characteristics, but trying to explain them to you means using only ordinary and inadequate words. I found the Lord to be loyal, pure, incorruptible, unchanging, constant, trustworthy, peaceful, giving, and faithful, and He was a provider of love with absolutely no conditions.

That want of a partner and husband was never far away. The desire for someone to love me was deeply entrenched in my heart. I didn't want to lie down and give up, but this place that I'd come to and the journey I'd been on had left me at a dead end.

I'm not going to say that I thought all men were terrible; however, if questioned during certain portions of my life, that answer might have varied. I knew there were a few good and kind men, but I viewed those few as exceptions.

During my thirty years of working, the majority of that time was spent in a male-dominated career. Over that period of time I was around hundreds of men who served in all capacities for varying lengths of time. I began to believe there were many more men who weren't good and kind than the number of those who were. There just seemed so few men willing to invest themselves, their time, and their love into their families. "Husbands, love your wives, just as Christ loved the church and gave himself up for her" (Ephesians 5:25 NIV).

Honestly I didn't know why I had this insatiable want for a partner, but I did. No matter how much I tried to hide it and put it down, the want would come right back up to the surface. I never liked being alone, and now I'd thrown away all my chances. All my options were gone. My bed was still empty, and so was my heart.

How could I have thought I could make good decisions in any part of my life when it involved a man? I'd come to believe that the majority of men weren't trustworthy, and many of them were cheaters and liars. So what was it that kept me wanting and looking? I had no solutions. Ultimately I wasn't even sure God could get me out of this one. But then again I was only able to look at it from my perspective.

It was several years later before I began to become more knowledgeable about all the words my new friend had shared. So many changes had been brought to me, and the Lord was making Himself very evident in my life. I began to wonder if it really was possible that God could step into the role of a husband in my life. Maybe, just maybe, then I wouldn't be so lonely.

This became my dilemma or what I came to think of as a quandary. I set out toward my next step of learning as much about that type of connection as I could. I found that God desires for you to consider a relationship with Him to be serious and binding. With my research, I began to understand my relationship with God really would become much like an earthly marriage. There would be commitments of fidelity, love, and trust. I already knew He loved me, but now I was beginning to actually sense it and embrace that feeling. It's as if He was drawing me to Him because He was so unyielding, and I felt an underlying trust being slowly generated.

I began to understand this marital relationship with God brings with it, His desire for you to be dependent on Him. He wants to fulfill all your desires, wants, and needs. Scripture indicates that an unmarried woman is as a virgin in respect to not belonging to any man or male husband. Therefore, God has a right to an expectation of physical celibacy. He requires faithfulness in this relationship because He indeed considers it a union. God has definitely provided multiple teachings and Scriptures regarding sexual sin, including adultery and fornication. Even though your union with Him will not be of a sexual nature, He expects you to behave morally and within His guidelines as if it were.

In giving to Him your acceptance of His authority and responsibility as a husband to you, that means you're agreeing to the expectations. He yearns for you to keep Him first above all others, upholding your commitment in the same sacredness as an earthly marriage. God's expectation demands you not give yourself or your body away.

As your husband, God wants to care for you, bless you, protect and defend you, take away your fears, remove feelings of inadequacy, place over you a covering of blessings, and provide love unconditionally. I found letting the Lord be your husband and casting your cares upon Him allows for freedom and gifts to you an opportunity for a future.

It wasn't apparent at the very beginning, but not long after I'd made my decision to go ahead and trust God to be my husband, I realized I wasn't feeling lonely anymore. That in itself was a total miracle, and it began a series of revelations into how God was working in my life.

God began filling in all those needy spaces in my life with His peace, and the depth of His love pacified the core of me. That unconditional love He was giving to me felt as if everyday I could sense it more. I began to understand that He really is all you'll ever need, and you'll eventually realize that's more than enough.

The words my new Christian friend had said to me so long before had just been fulfilled. He'd said, "When you realize how much Jesus loves you, you won't need the love of a man." So I can tell you by example that it's not about how much you love Him. It's about how much you believe He loves you.

I was surprised when I became aware that my needs and wants had changed. I no longer felt unloved. Nor was I feeling a lack in any personal areas of my life. By the time you begin to realize all of this, God's proven to you that He can be counted on and is definitely trustworthy.

The way in which He loves you is so complete that lack and void isn't even a consideration. When you find yourself understanding the Lord has become your best partner, you'll want to safeguard your relationship, tuck that sense of Him and that awareness of Him right into your heart, and take Him everywhere you go. Don't leave Him out. Confide in Him over all your concerns and enjoy the liberty and openness of your life. When you have the kind of relationship where you can open up your thoughts and speak freely, knowing you'll never be discounted because of it, what could be better than that?

For those of you who are divorced, are widowed, or never married, I want to stress I have learned firsthand that the Lord actually can be your spiritual husband. If you're a believer, you can have a significant relationship with Him. He's available every moment, seven days a week, twelve months a year, for the entire time you're on earth. The wonderful present you get from the Lord is complete confidence in knowing that He is there for you in any situation and that He's chosen His best just for you.

During my years of marriage and separations, my sexual life was, for lack of a better term, hit and miss. I had wanted that in my life, but that wasn't something I was going to get in a marriage relationship with the Lord. Let me tell you. This one was a big one for me. I was so worried that this was going to take an overwhelmingly huge amount of faith, endurance, resistance, and rebuking. But I have to willingly confess that the Lord proved me to be in error.

It took a while, and for most of that time I whined to the Lord about how unfair it was. But the closer I drew to Him, the more I learned about Him. It just became something that slowly lost its strength and became easier to overcome. At first it was stronger than normal. It was like a new diet, and I had to deal with it daily and fight cravings all the time. But God had me so completely covered that those urges and emotions just kind of fell away. Now every once in a while I'll have that occasional thought, but it's easy to cast down. I've never felt that I had a loss, and to me this is nothing short of a miracle! "For I am convinced that neither death nor life, neither angels nor demons, neither the present nor the future, nor any powers, neither height nor depth, nor anything else in all creation, will be able to separate us from the love of God that is in Christ Jesus our Lord" (Romans 8:38–39 NIV).

As that woman who made many wrong decisions in her life, I had found it an easy road to become discouraged and insecure about a future. My basic personality was more timid than strong, and as I mentioned before, I was the one who always assisted those in need. I didn't pull for myself, and I didn't give myself the option of putting myself first. I gave in a lot to pressure, and I would give over my opinion of what I personally thought was best because it just seemed nicer or easier or less chaotic.

It was a way of living life, making wrong choices, living with the consequences, and feeling like that was not going to change. Too many wrong steps compounded with more wrong steps had left me heavy, and I felt like I had little self-worth.

If you don't believe you're worthy, no amount of counseling or teaching or attempts at change will permanently work. You absolutely have to grab onto the fact that God believes in you and He wants you. He knit you together in your mother's womb. He designed you and gave you your personality and what makes you unique. Even though God knows you have issues, He sees you as worthy, and that doesn't come by anything you do. Your worth and your righteousness comes from Christ's sacrificial giving of His life and blood. Don't deny what the Lord has done for you. Accept that you're a new creature in Christ. The old things are gone, and all things have become new. "How much more, then, will the blood of Christ, who through the eternal Spirit offered himself unblemished to God, cleanse our consciences from acts that lead to death, so that we may serve the living God" (Hebrews 9:14 NIV). "Therefore, if anyone is in Christ, the new creation has come: The old has gone, the new is here" (2 Corinthians 5:17 NIV).

When I began to understand more about the necessity of healing in my heart and accepted how this could benefit my commitment with the Lord, I found myself drawn to the New Testament, specifically John 4. This chapter is about a conversation that Jesus had one very warm afternoon with a Samaritan woman at a community well.

Being a Samaritan meant she wasn't allowed to associate with Jewish society, and because of her past and present marital state, she was an outsider with her own people. She had come to the well in the heat of the day and was alone.

When Jesus approached her, He asked her for a drink. This would definitely not have been a normal request for Jesus, as a Jew. She immediately questioned Him about why He had asked her. Then He told her that if she knew the gift of God and who it was who was asking her for a drink, she would have asked Him, and He would have given her living water.

Without her saying anything first, Jesus explained that He knew she had had five husbands and the man she was with now was not her husband. They continued in their conversation, and He began to talk about the difference between the water of the well and His living water. He then attempted to explain that drinking from her well would only result in her being thirsty over and over. He then enlightened her to the fact that drinking from His living water meant she would never thirst again. Jesus explained to her that this living water would become as a spring welling up to eternal life.

By letting her know that when He sat down with her, He already knew of her situation with men, He was implying that she held worth. It was a sort of declaration to her that He knew all about her but still cared enough to want to give her help. Her testimony to her fellow citizens that day was that Jesus had told her everything she'd ever done.

The interaction Jesus has with this woman speaks volumes about His compassion and the value He places on her regardless of her gender, her race, or her mistakes. He desired for her to understand that if she truly thirsted after this living spiritual water, she would have to give up the burden of her sins. Basically Jesus was giving her the opportunity to let go of her failed relationships. She had been looking for something they could never give to her. She needed a love with no conditions, and trusting in people to meet that kind of need only exposed her to failure because no earthly man could have ever lived up to that expectation.

I can totally understand now that analogy when I apply it in my life. I always drank from the wrong well. After my one experience at the age of sixteen, praying for God's guidance in my life and accepting what He had shown me, I had never again let the Lord have the ultimate decision regarding men. If I prayed, I'd then move ahead into my own decision, always stopping short. I can almost visualize the Lord standing there and waiting for me to finish my delivered speech. Then mere days would go by before I would make my decision to just go ahead. That's what I did. I just went. I kept that pattern of drinking from that same well, and the Lord would just let me because I never waited for Him. Oh, how I should have waited for my God to bring me to the water from the right well.

Because God's purpose and intention has always been bent on eternity, when He created Adam, it was never His desire that man would die. It was always supposed to be Adam and Eve and God in the garden of Eden. God's supposed to be first above all others, but I believe He wants to also be in the center of all your relationships.

In all the references I checked on the Web regarding biblical numbers, they all indicated that the number three is given as a symbol of completeness and perfection. An example of this would be the Trinity. The Holy Trinity is made up of God the Father, God the Son, and God the Holy Spirit. It seems reasonable to me that a cord made of three strands is just simply much stronger. "A cord of three strands is not quickly broken" (Ecclesiastes 4:12 NIV).

When Adam and Eve chose to go against what God had told them, they sinned and lost that relationship bond and eventually did die. On our own humans simply cannot be trusted to always love and always put God and His will in the center of our lives.

This woman at the well had wanted her husbands to make her feel complete, but a spouse can basically only meet your secondary need, not your primary need. It's unfair to assume that any human can meet your needs for a length of time called, forever. They can't truthfully tell you that they won't ever fail you or that they'll always have your best interest at heart. They also can't in reality promise they'll never ignore you or even leave you. Jesus is the only one who can do that. He says He won't ever physically turn away. Nor will He take His heart away from you. On your worst day Jesus will still accept you, and that's forever.

If you don't openly trust God to meet your personal needs, then you'll automatically transfer those expectations to the people closest to you. That begins a dependency on each other, but God should be your only source for that. He's your hope. They're not. Wouldn't it be better to put yourself in God's hands and let Him give you the unconditional love and then just enjoy your human husband for the attributes he has? The woman at the well wanted to have the husband meet her deepest needs. I imagine it caused huge stress between them because that's a futile, never-ending battle. She continued indulging marriage after marriage after marriage with no real hope. She shouldn't have expected them to fill those holes in her life in the way that she needed and wanted. They were never going to be able to fill her heart to its capacity and overflowing.

I know that because I was her. I went from relationship to relationship, never feeling satisfied. Something within me was always missing. I didn't know what it was, but looking at it now, I can see clearly that I just needed to let go and be in love with God.

Thank the Lord that He is rich in His promises. He's full of mercy and grace and gives to you the desires of your heart. Rely on Him for your every need and let Him be your protector and defender. Let Him take your fears away and be your confidant and the love of your life. Don't worry about your next earthly relationship until you and the Lord have yours all set up and running. You'll never get it right until that Jesus-size hole in your heart gets filled up with

Him. Remember—a husband would have that same need for Jesus in his heart, and you won't be able to fill him up either. God made you guys that way. He put that place for Jesus inside you when He made you in your mother's womb, and He's the only one who can and will fill it.

Chapter

25

Healings Past and Present

Many years ago I remember being involved with a group of women, and they began talking about the past and how much it troubled them. The majority of the talk revolved around the pain of remembering and their wish that they could go back and change it. I definitely fell right into line with their thinking because my past was filled with much regret. But I knew there was no way to change what had happened, so I decided to just not think about it more than I had to.

One day my new Christian friend casually stated to me during a conversation that God was big in the business of healing. My ears perked up, and I started asking questions because I loved talking about healing of the body. My life certainly wasn't squared away, but I definitely had a huge faith and belief for healings. We talked for a long time that day, and the conversation ended with his mention that God could heal anyone and anything, including someone's past. I thought a lot about that conversation in the weeks that followed. I began to wonder about the possibility and realized that if it was true, that would be pretty cool. But your past has involved lots of other people, so what would that actually mean for them and the part they'd played?

Believe it or not, this topic came back at least three or more times during future discussions with him. It was only later that I found out this was a regular tactic that the Holy Spirit used to get my attention when He wanted me to listen. It was kind of like He was dropping spiritual hints.

One afternoon about six months later I was sitting and talking with an old friend, and I actually found myself saying that God could heal her past. Those words just tumbled right out of my own mouth, and when I said them, it surprised me. That's when I realized I must somehow actually believe the words I'd just said. Somewhere along the way, my heart had taken ownership of that concept. I certainly had never had trouble believing in healing of the physical body, but now I believed in the healing of a person's past. I mean that wasn't even a body part. It was such a huge stretch in my faith, so I decided I needed to begin to investigate this idea further.

I had thought there were probably multitudes of people who lived good Christian lives but had been forced to endure some type of abuse. I figured because they hadn't been the problem themselves, they were good candidates for that type of healing. I certainly couldn't conjure up a situation where someone like me would be worthy of that. I hadn't acted correctly, and I had trouble not repeating the same behaviors and making the same wrong decisions.

It's a hard concept to relay to someone else, but I really didn't contemplate or wonder about this healing for me. It didn't cross my mind. It didn't roll around in my head. It didn't hurt my heart, and bother me when I thought others could have this healing and I couldn't. I didn't feel left out. I just didn't really put myself in as the patient. If you don't believe you're worthy enough for others to care about you, then why would you presume a promise of something of that magnitude?

I knew God set His path before me, but He also gave me the ability to make my own choices. It's been my belief that consequences are the outcome of wrong choices and bad decisions. After years of divorcing and remarrying, I still had no husband. I was lonely and fearful. I had no social partner and no one with whom to set goals and dream. So a healing for what I'd done to myself would not ever have been up for thought or discussion.

I always knew when I asked for forgiveness of my sins that because I felt repentant, I was forgiven. But that didn't change how I felt about any of the residual effects of my previous behavior. I'm talking about those consequences. They're real. They're alive. They're feeling good about themselves and working in your life.

Praise God for my new Christian friend, and thank you Jesus that he continued to pray for me and give me good counsel and feed me hope. Little by little I saw that something different, something exciting and life changing could happen. Applying the theory of that type of healing to my life would never have been possible without my trustable friend putting that seed of thought out there where my heart could take possession.

So after I spouted out that statement to my girlfriend about God being able to heal a past, I began to think about the possibility of giving myself a break and praying about it for me. I knew the only way a healing could take place for something as devastating and crippling as an ugly past was if it came straight from God. My assumption was that it would probably take a lot of time for it to be fixed because I had spent a lot of time making it. I wasn't sure I was ready, but I knew for my own personal health I had to allow myself to try. I needed to accept new thinking and be able to throw out the old. My future or what I believed I had left of it suddenly became very important, and I became determined to let the Lord have the lead this time.

So I asked God to show me what I needed to do and what I might need to step away from. I admitted to Him I had no idea how it was going to work or what it really involved. My decision that day was to do my best to have faith and to trust God, and I was willing to allow Him to do whatever it took, no matter the cost. I wanted to become that person I should have been, not the person I had become, a person with a future, not one with just a past.

In that decision I soon became aware that the Holy Spirit fully intended to walk right along with me when I was facing all those issues and help me figure it out as we went. In praying about this, I discovered that my attempt to stuff things way into the back of my mind and my heart hadn't done anything but cause me to hold on to anger and frustration. I didn't know that tucking things inside would end in eruptions that multiplied and festered. By getting it out into the open, it could be taken apart piece by piece, aired out, cleaned out, and conquered. I wanted to discontinue my pattern of being vulnerable to treating the people presently in my life as if they were the responsible culprits.

The Holy Spirit, the third divine person of the Trinity, helps guide you, teach you, prompt you, and empower you. He leads you one step at a time into the truth that sets you free. Why hadn't I known earlier that all I had to do to become free of my past was to listen and obey?

Just as my new friend had tried to tell me, I became convinced that letting God be what I needed Him to be was definitely a great way to get started. Still it was very confusing. I wasn't sure yet exactly who that was. In thinking it over one night, I decided a good way to begin was to give the Lord one of my biggest problems and ask for help. So I decided to give Him my problem of being afraid of the dark and the unknown and then ask Him to be my protector and deliver me from my fear. After all, hadn't my friend said God could be anything I needed? I'd been plagued my entire life with a severe fear of the dark, and that fear had stolen my sense of ease during the nighttime hours. Consequently I'd done more time sleeping on the couch than criminals had done in prison for robbing banks.

I'd always had my own rationale for the reason I slept on the couch. I told myself I could protect my children better if I surrendered myself to the intruder first. But honestly I knew myself, and there was just no way I could be in a bed in a contained room and listen to every sound the house made. Every noise gave me cause to assume it wasn't going to turn out well. Yep, at that point in my life the couch was as safe as I could get.

For much of my adult life I'd had no physical protector I could count on, and my fear of the dark and the unknown made night barely tolerable. Of course there was always some kind of weapon close by, but my real hope was that intruders would leave the very moment I started screaming. My theory of a weapon never made much sense either. I wanted my weapon dangerous enough to hurt intruders but not so dangerous that if they overpowered me and took it, they could kill me with it.

Sometimes I wonder if the Lord ever shakes His head and chuckles over some of the stuff we think, say, and do. I'd watched my kids when they were little and my sister's children as they grew up, and I got lots and lots of giggles from the most ridiculous things they said and did. So who knows? Maybe when God is watching all of us say and do those same ridiculous things, He gets that same smile on His face as our daddy God.

After I gave to the Lord an explanation of my fear, I then felt it was necessary to give Him a further understanding of how really seriously afraid I was. I thought if I really told Him how bad it was, He would surely feel responsible to absolutely take care of it for me. I hadn't really pieced it all together, and I didn't know how to just give God something as all-encompassing as my fear of the dark. That fear had ruled my life for all of my life, how do you just let go of that? I had no idea how that was even possible, but what I didn't realize was that the Lord already knew all my fears and every emotion I had regarding them. I also hadn't figured out that God would have done all that for me just because He loved me, not because I had convinced Him of anything. I didn't realize I didn't have to make it all dark and scary to Him. All I had to do was ask.

So that's what I finally did. I bundled it all up in my head and then presented the bundle to the Lord. Determination hit me, and I was resolved to trust Him to be my protector and do my best to believe He would. Then for good measure I asked Him to help me trust Him to do that. It took me so long to figure out that all I had to do to begin that process was just ask. I get so tied up in giving my reasons for everything I do, but God didn't want them. He just wanted me to need Him and ask Him. "I waited patiently for the LORD; he turned to me and heard my cry. He lifted me out of the slimy pit, out of the mud and mire; he set my feet on a rock and gave me a firm place to stand. He put a new song in my mouth, a hymn of praise to our God. Many will see and fear the LORD and put their trust in him" (Psalm 40:1–3 NIV).

Now that I had done that, I felt I was ready to take my first baby step. I knew my worst time was the dead of night. That's the time when everyone should be sleeping, and it's easier for intruders to make their way into your dwelling without being heard or noticed.

So I decided I would let myself fall asleep on the couch while I was watching television. When I woke up during the night, I'd get up and flip on a light or two or three while I made my way to my own bed. I was hoping that would be a hint to all the random robbers and deviants that someone was home.

I started out doing this, but I was still spending most of the night on the couch. A long time after I would get up and go to my bed, I would still be awake, waiting and listening. I'd listen to my house creak, to the noise of my neighbors, to the wind blowing in the bushes, and to vehicles that sounded like they were doing slow drive-by's past my house. I mean, are you aware that new ice plunking into the freezer bin sounds eerily the same as someone knocking against your door? In the dark everything is different, and all is imaginable. For months I consistently reminded God that He had told me He would do this and that I was really counting on Him.

It was extremely challenging in the beginning because fear is such a big boogeyman when you let it be. Even though I knew I wasn't a real threat to anyone who wanted to gain access to my house, I still knew I could be counted on to try to ward away evil. In giving that up and relying solely on the Lord, most people would think that to be awesome. But to me it was all about losing control. I had just given all of that away.

After I moved out of my parents' home, I don't believe there was ever a time when I totally counted on anyone for the protection of me or my kids. In the back of my mind I always knew I would be there just in case someone let me down, whether on purpose or by accident. That's why this whole ordeal was terribly forbidding to me.

Becoming a follower doesn't necessarily mean you just let everyone run your life however they want, although they will try. I think for me it was more an issue of my need to borrow someone else's self-confidence when I was placed in circumstances outside my circle of comfort. However, in my own internal life it was vital that I established control of what I was capable of controlling. It's rather like picking out something and then standing your ground and not letting go for anyone. There has to be something in the lives of *followers* that they alone can grab onto and that they're not willing to allow someone else to take from them. I know God understood this, and honestly somehow when I asked for Him to help me to trust Him, He did just that. I don't know how, but He did do it. And my trust did grow greater. I eventually became able to sleep more and more without fear.

In the beginning when noises would wake me up, I learned to say a little prayer. After that happened like two thousand times, I realized I'd memorized that prayer, and every time it happened, I'd say, "Thank You, Jesus, for being my defender and protector and my guide. Thank You for keeping away all the things that would scare me or hurt me or kill me and for keeping away all the bad spiritual things." The routine happened so often that even if I woke out of a sound sleep, I'd automatically start that sentence, and these few years later I still continue that practice. Sometimes the prayer is longer, but usually it's the same.

It was vitally important for me to get this. It had been a strategic move for me to begin with one of the biggest negatives in my entire life. It had ruled me, taken my peace, and left me feeling like a target. I came to realize that the Lord was waiting for me to be as serious in my quest as He was in answering it.

I won't bore you with all the details, but I will tell you this process took me months and months. I didn't say it took God, I said it took me months and months and months. My fear of the dark and the unknown had been there from my earliest memory, and it was a favorite strategy of the enemy. But my God repeatedly has proven Himself to me and has protected me. He has guarded me, and I no longer have that cloud of fear. I do find periodically that a fearful moment will rise up in me. But then I just go back to my faith prayer, and it goes away. Every time that happens and the fear immediately disappears, I gain more strength of faith. God knows I depend on Him alone for my safety, my daily comfort, and my defense. He would never let me down. He has proved over and over that He truly can be trusted and that He will be to me anything I need Him to be.

When you finally decide to let the Lord begin a spiritual healing surgery in your life and with your past, something miraculous will happen. I had called on God to prove Himself, and He had. I had always tried to overcome these crazy fears on my own, and every time I tried, I failed. The concept of letting God be God and be who He really is, along with believing that He really will do what He says, was something I knew about in head-knowledge only. I'd heard it before, but actually giving over to Him my issues of fear and then letting Him do it, was brand new for me. The healing the Lord brought to my life was phenomenal, and I can't even express the freedom I've begun to enjoy.

One of the names of God is *Jehovah-Rapha*, which means Healer. I've learned that many of the Scriptures in the Bible reveal Him as a healer of physical, emotional, and spiritual wounds, and many people refer to Him as our Great Physician. He knows your pain, the ugly stuff, and all the memories of dark things. When He readies you for healing, He begins to prepare your heart, mind, and spirit so that His heavenly remedies can do their job. He will clean out the contaminated and sore areas of your life, including your past. He gives medicinal doses of calmness, peace, freedom, and security. Because He loves you so much, He adds in a little self-respect and a further knowledge of Him. There won't be any gaps or holes left if you let Him and give Him permission to take care of them.

Over time you'll find that memories of your past are still there, but the pain and all of the shame and guilt that was associated with those memories are gone. You can use those memories and any leftover scars as a witness for others. These can teach them about the mighty power of the Lord and of His loving and tender care of you. One of the best people to help someone else get help is the person who has already been through this process and has come out on the other side victorious.

Don't forget to remind those you're helping that whenever the Lord is working in your life, you can expect that enemy, the devil, to also try to undermine what's being done. He doesn't want the Lord to be your everything. He wants that to be his territory. He wants total control of you, and he will wreak havoc, seeking devastation and your emotional and spiritual death. This adversary works through your thoughts and memories.

After the Lord heals your past, any memories you have are just going to be memories. It's like they have a significance in your life, but they don't hold hurtful emotion or pain. But if you haven't gotten healed yet and you allow the enemy to travel that road and bring you to the past, he'll bring that pain and sorrow right along with him. He knows your trigger points, and he'll bring everything against you he can. Remember—part of his warfare is his initial act of finding out if you're going to allow him to set you up. Don't give him that satisfaction. Don't let him be in control of your emotions, behavior, and moods. Kick him out, tell him to get lost, and don't spend any time on anything he's brought to you. Cast it away.

The enemy wants to consume all the good he can until he achieves his goal of taking your peace and your victory. He hates you, and he desires to trash and defeat your very existence. He knows you're a believer and you have the Holy Spirit inside of you. If he can keep you from listening to the Holy Spirit, he knows his chances are better. He'll continue to move in your life, sometimes in waves, leaving you alone and then hitting hard. Don't give in easily. Ask the Holy Spirit to let you know when he's around. Be aware that if you let him, he'll weigh you down with depression, job losses, divorces, the loss of your home, and even the loss of your health. Do not underestimate him.

All those negatives in your life will become available as targets for him to make you believe the Lord is the one responsible. He'll offer up questions so that you ask why the Lord would let that happen to you. If he can cause a divorce and take your money, home, and health, he's hoping you'll be overwhelmed with depression, throw in the towel, and blame God.

I've heard sick people say so many times, "Why is God doing this to me?" It's not God. God doesn't cause sickness, and He doesn't work in the negative. He would not have allowed Jesus to sacrifice Himself on the cross and take on His back all the sins, diseases, infirmities, and the condemnation just to turn around and give them back to you.

Once the enemy has you on the run, he can't really back off until he achieves his desired goal because he knows the Lord is working on your behalf. It all started when the serpent began to talk with Eve. He came to her and presented a scenario regarding the tree in the center of the garden of Eden. God had instructed them not to eat from it and said if they did, they would surely die. The serpent questioned Eve about that, and then Eve allowed herself to reflect on it and wonder. She should have stopped him right there when the serpent began to speak to her about something that God had already instructed them about. Eve should have taken her authority and sent that serpent down the road, but she didn't. It's my belief that by the time the enemy came toward Eve clothed in a serpent suit, he had already taken as much time as he needed in his study of her. He apparently sensed vulnerability, and so he took his opportunity to deceive and manipulate her.

Scripture says the enemy comes into your life and he attempts to kill, steal, and destroy. He will take everything you *let* him have. He'll take it all if you allow it. It's imperative to maintain the well-being of your spirit because that's your way to oppose the flesh. When I say flesh, I mean your desires, your sinful acts, your obedience to the opposite of God's nature. If you let the enemy take you into a state of opposition, depression, oppression, and failure, your faith has little chance of survival. When you walk with the Lord and speak in faith and authority with Scripture, that's when the enemy is forced to stop. When Christ left the earth, He gave you authority to overcome all the power of the enemy, and then He left you the Comforter, Holy Spirit, to help. The Holy Spirit is the third part of the Trinity. As a spirit, He dwells within you. He empowers you and gives you the ability to carry out God's will in your life. "Then Jesus came to them and said, 'All authority in heaven and on earth has been given to me'" (Matthew 28:18 NIV). "If you love me, keep my commands. And I will ask the Father, and he will give you another advocate to help you and be with you forever … But the Advocate, the Holy Spirit, whom the Father will send in my name, will teach you all things and will remind you of everything I have said to you" (John 14:15–16, 26 NIV).

As I review all the changes that have occurred in my life, I remember one thing taking a long time for me to understand. It was the fact that if I kept repeating the same behaviors and not changing anything, I would go on having the same trials over and over and over. That repetition meant I was missing something important that I needed for correction and for healing. I'm sure the Holy Spirit had been attempting to get me to figure that one out, but I just didn't. I was all twisted up, and I didn't have any spiritual vision for the future. I didn't have enough knowledge or truth to even know that this spiraling of bad choices and resulting behavior could stop and that changes could then occur. If you're desirous of a healing of your heart and your mind, it's inevitable that you'll have to make that step back into your past. If you want freedom from fear, just ask Him. You may not be fearful of the dark, but you may be fearful of many other things. Make yourself available to listen to what the Holy Spirit says to you and then apply it to your life. Remember fear comes from a sense of powerlessness and your inability to control the outcome. The Lord says fear is the opposite of faith because it means you either don't trust in what Jesus says or you don't trust Him to perform what He says. Defeat your fears by remembering that through Christ, He has made you a conqueror. Once you know, once it's in your heart, then God's able to move you to a higher level, and you'll never again find yourself subject to destruction by fear. Fear may present itself, but destruction by fear won't happen. Once you've tucked that into your heart solidly, it brings forth light. Much like the old drug dealer, the enemy can't traffic in the light or what is known as truth. The enemy can only traffic in darkness or what is called ignorance of truth. Do not let yourself be ignorant of truth. Put on your armor, study God's Word, memorize several key Scriptures, and then be on the ready. "Have nothing to do with the fruitless deeds of darkness, but rather expose them" (Ephesians 5:11 NIV).

After Christ's sacrifice on the cross, there was nothing left that could separate you and God. Once you accept Him, you can have that one-on-one relationship with Him. Christ was your redemption. He took all the ugly, and He paid the full price. How much more could He demonstrate His love for you? You've been washed in His blood and have been made righteous through Him. When you know that you're in Christ and He is within you, you can face your fears and your past with confidence, and He will turn it all into victory.

Chapter
26

Is This My Life?

There are times in life when you find that patterns of behavior or addictions of all kinds have somehow made their way into your life. Often by the time you recognize them as problems, they've already become entrenched in the functioning portion of living.

It's just possible that because you were wading through life, you didn't recognize any symptoms or warning signs from the Holy Spirit. These promptings would have allowed you to understand you were giving up your control little by little.

If you've begun thinking the enemy always works in the same way, I believe you may want to rethink that. The enemy is in a battle, so he's not going to give away his position. Nor is he going to let you know his real goal. If he's attempting to develop a slow infusion of behavior change or working to get you further involved in an addiction, his tactics will be sneaky, calculating, sly, inventive, and low to the ground.

There've been times in my life when I wasn't guarded. I hadn't realized that over a period of time my general conduct and train of thought had begun to slip a little. I've heard others tell the same story about how they'd let this modern world and its liberal views become embedded into their lives. They admitted they hadn't even realized that slow progression.

So it's not only possible, but it's probable that without watching and having a firm grasp on your spiritual walk, things could easily slip in without you noticing. It would be like jumping to the assumption that the number two always comes directly after the number one. When you make that assumption, you feel released from the need to continue to pay attention. But does number two always come right after number one? What about one and a half? Could it show up once in a while? That answer is a definite yes, but did it cross your mind? Take caution and watch for those little numbers in between your jumps in life. They might be the important concerns. They look little and easily fit in without you noticing, but that's what makes them dangerous. The enemy hasn't taken down millions of people by slacking off in his job, so be guarded.

Your future is something the enemy wants, and he will go to great lengths to prevent you from fulfilling the purpose for which God designed you. He knows that if he can get you to continually battle things in your life like habits, addictions, vocabulary, and fleshly desires, you'll be so busy overcoming that you'll never really overcome. Keep that strong line of defense. Don't let yourself be available to what everyone throws out as their opinion and don't automatically use their standards for your own guide. Be strong in your own values and beliefs.

When I began writing this manual, I decided that I'd be totally honest. I knew I had to continually add in anything I believed the Holy Spirit was prompting me to say. I also knew that I was being called to just put it all out there for everyone to see. In my heart

I knew that if I gave it all to you and didn't withhold secrets or embarrassing places in my life, I could bring a truth to your life.

During years when Husband #2 and I were separated and while my children were teenagers, I got involved with a routine that I believed to be totally harmless. By that time in my life we'd already decided to have separate bank accounts, and I was working in a job that was paying fairly well. My teenage kids had young lives of their own, so my time was pretty open. One night my friend called and asked me to go with her to play high-stakes bingo. It was local and not very far away, so I decided to go with her, and that night I won $600. I'd had a lot of fun, and it seemed totally harmless, so I agreed to go with her again that next week.

I like numbers, so I enjoyed the basics of the game of bingo, and of course, everyone enjoys being able to win money. It wasn't long before I began going even when my friend couldn't go. I won more times than I lost, and that in its self was exciting. But the other satisfaction came with the thrill of the chase of that one number that made you a winner.

My routine of playing bingo continued well after my children were gone from home. My marriage had been over for quite some time, and because I basically had no social life, my girlfriend and I began traveling on the weekends. Many times we'd go over to Nevada for short trips to gamble. I soon became fascinated with the slots because their keno machines were very similar to bingo. I could pick my own numbers to play, and of course, I believed that was to my advantage.

I absolutely didn't realize that the addicting joy and excitement of winning would cause an actual addiction to the gambling itself. I'd always felt in control of my money, and I had set aside certain amounts (designated as entertainment) to use when I played. I don't think I even realized that my entertainment fund was getting larger—that is, not until toward the end.

Overall I won a lot of money, but over the course of the long haul, like many others, I came out on the losing end. Even though the losing began to come more often than the winning, I still felt a very compelling desire, to gamble. That want, tugs and pulls at your thoughts about trying just one more time, giving it one more chance to win. You consistently think that if you wait it out, your luck will change and you can pay yourself back what you've spent. That's about the time when the addiction in your life brings more of an overwhelming feeling of defeat, coercion, craving, and a whole lot less excitement.

Don't assume that bingo, keno, or even the lotto won't take you there. It's all a form of gambling, and gambling is an iffy proposition. If left unopposed, that habit will continue to gain in strength, and it will become a stronghold in your life. That stronghold will beat you up and leave you for dead.

Even writing this portion of my story is bringing up memories and emotions. I feel a gut-level excitement welling up. It's as if my own self is trying to convince me that it would be okay for me now to hop in the car and just go gamble. But I'm not going, and I am never giving in again. I'm resolved to the fact that it was a stronghold to me. I'm firm in my belief that strongholds are designed by the enemy. It's that hook in your jaw, and you've just become the *catch of the day*.

Please take this as a caution. These last paragraphs are the truth, and they alone should remind you that the enemy is never far away and that he never gets tired.

You know God knows everything. When you get before Him to talk about your issues and you begin to explain the things you've done, that stuff isn't a surprise to Him. He already knows all about you, and yet He still wants you to come to Him. Don't let that connection, that concept slip by you. I believe His purpose in wanting you to talk with Him is simply so He can be there for you.

When you repent and ask forgiveness for all the sins you've committed, He takes them and tosses them away like you do when you throw out the garbage. Don't ever believe the lies of the enemy when he says you have to continue to feel bad over what you've done. Why would you ever feel badly about something that's not there anymore? God doesn't have them in His memory bank or in His vault. They're gone, never to be remembered. That's a movement on God's behalf that will absolutely allow you as a believer of Christ the freedom to begin again.

God's method of operation doesn't include making you wait until you can quit what you're doing to come before Him. In fact, it's really just the opposite because God wants you to come to Him so that He can help you quit what you're doing.

As a believer, the Lord wants you to know behavior and addictions don't define who you really are inside. When you're trying to walk by faith into being free and you fall back into sinful behavior or addiction, immediately call out to God and yell for help. Don't let that temporary barrier produce in you a want to give up on the whole campaign.

I can't tell you how many times I've broken my own eating program and then immediately became frustrated. I'd get mad for giving in and then just walk around telling myself it was over because I'd just blown it. Then because I knew I'd blown it, I would just continue on and keep eating poorly all day. The Holy Spirit has been showing me that I've actually been allowing myself to use that one bad food choice to be my excuse to continue to eat badly. If I would just recognize that I blew it and then stop and think about it,

I'd be able to continue that day without further damage. The trick is understanding that it's your sinful flesh that wants to continue in what it wants to do, and now it has an excuse. The other side of that trick is knowing that you don't have to listen to your sinful flesh.

So when you experience those times of failure, listen for the promptings of the Holy Spirit, listen to what He tells you. Do whatever it takes to remove yourself from whatever situation took you there. Don't hesitate at all. Immediately plead for God's help, pouring your heart out, and do that out loud if you can. I find it's more effective if I speak to Him just like I would another person. It gives it intent, a type of strength-filled purpose. It's like adding exclamation points to your sentence. "For as high as the heavens are above the earth, so great is his love for those who fear him; as far as the east is from the west, so far has he removed our transgressions from us" (Psalm 103:11–12 NIV).

It's so vital that you grasp the importance of just admitting and confessing what you're thinking and what you're doing. That's not because you should feel a constant state of guilt all the time. It's because you need to understand what you've been doing and hopefully why you've been doing it. When you say your words out loud, it makes it more visible to your mind. It makes it real. This is not the time to be sticking your head in the ground and ignoring what's going on.

God says He puts a desire for Himself within every person. Now what I'm going to say next is my own personal view. When I think about that empty spot for God within me, I visualize it as a type of vortex similar to those in the space movies. The space or the void would have a swirling pull toward its center like a whirlpool. Now the Lord intended for that gap or that space to be filled with Him, but many times people try to fill it with fleshly desires. They think they know what will make them happy, so they search for the things they believe they want and allow those things to get pulled into that open place. Many times the stuff they're drawn toward includes lust, alcohol, greed, drugs, gambling, self-gratification, and indulgences. Don't fill that God-shaped space with garbage or with the sin of flesh and all the wrong things because then there's no room left for Him. If you always remember to fill up on God first, then you won't have that same harsh hunger for the appetites of the flesh. You won't have desires pulling on you because through a personal relationship with Jesus, that God-shaped hole becomes filled to overflowing with Him and His blessings.

So when you feel that drawing and pulling to continue your sinful pleasure, stop for a second and ask yourself, "What is it that's wooing me and drawing me back? What's causing a change and beginning that pull on my life?" Try and get that nailed down, and then you can confront it. Ask God for the miracle of healing and then for a total release from that grip on your life.

It may be that because you're trying to take back the control, now the enemy is fighting you for it. *Do not* try to battle the enemy all by yourself. The Lord says to give Him your burdens. He didn't say to keep them and fight for them. So after you give God your ugly stuff, make sure you've got your spiritual armor on. Stand firm in your faith and let the Lord take over, following what He tells you to do.

Remember, even though it's all a spiritual battle at this point, these battles against the enemy can still cause you physical suffering. The enemy is desperate to draw you back into domination and anguish, and your feelings may tell you that you've lost your way. Don't ever give in to that. Access the Lord and tell Him what the enemy is doing. This is one time when it's okay to be a tattletale.

Chapter
27

The Real Deal

Making the Lord your *first* priority before anyone or anything else is a massive heart decision. It is, however, the one that will change your life forever. He's the one who formed you in your mother's womb and set a path and a plan for your life, one of promise and hope for the future.

God should be on your mind so much throughout your day that it feels like He's in the same room with you. He should be the first one you think of to call upon when you need help. He waits for you to pay attention to Him, and He so wants you to be that partner and companion.

Your God doesn't just love you. He's in love with you. He loves the whole of you, everything that makes you the person He created. He always hears your prayers, He's not too busy, and He's not irritated or annoyed with you. He might not answer your prayer the way you like or in the time limit you've set, but He will answer with His answer.

He's passionate about you and enthusiastic about having His love returned. God is your heavenly Father as well as your daddy God and everything in between. Give Him back your love, your belief in Him, your surrender, and your trust of Him. "'Then you will call on me and come and pray to me, and I will listen to you. You will seek me and find me when you seek me with all your heart. I will be found by you,' declares the LORD, 'and will bring you back from captivity" (Jeremiah 29:12–14 NIV).

As a believer, the Lord has called you into a relationship with Him. Generally a relationship exists between two people who are similar in resources. But in this relationship everything you have is because of God. None of this is only because of your own efforts. I can say that because it hasn't been created or authored by you. He's been the only Creator in this relationship. All of the talents and abilities of your life that helped you excel were imparted to you by God. He's the Creator. He made you, and everyone, and everything else. There is nothing that doesn't stem from His original creation. If something came from a particle taken from the dirt, it would still come from Him because He created the dirt. It's the same with the air, the water, and other human beings, all because they originated through God's creation. You can conceive an idea, formulate and design it, fabricate and construct it, but you can't create it. You can only take what God originally made and build from there.

When God created you, He not only put inside of you abilities and talents but also provided the necessary power, influence, and propensity for you to carry out those functions. Because He's a God who loves you, He gifts to you and bestows on your ministries favor and blessings. What a truly awesome God.

So if you're great at something, have a high intelligence, or have multiple talents, that's because your daddy God put that in you. You will probably spend years perfecting those talents and readying yourself to use your gifts, and that pleases God. That is actually one of

His objectives. That means you've taken the nucleus of His creation and put *you* into it. "For who makes you different from anyone else? What do you have that you did not receive? And if you did receive it, why do you boast as though you did not?" (1 Corinthians 4:7 NIV).

This relationship with God is designed for growth in your Christian life much like a child as he or she goes through life. When you're young and just learning, God doesn't require as much. As He grows you up and teaches you, He expects more. He wants you to eventually work in connection with Him so that you no longer expect Him to do everything for you. That means you're not in a helpless state because you've learned to trust what He's already taught you. That provides Him with a certain amount of trust He now can expect from you.

God then raises the standard in your life, or in simpler terms, He raises your goal to a higher level. Then He observes to see if you do the little things expected of you. Scripture says if you're faithful in the little things, He'll move you to the greater things. Whether you are the homemaker or you work in a factory, He expects you to still carry out the responsibility of being faithful and spiritually honorable.

At some point you may realize you don't have everything God's promised to you. That might be a good time to do some checking and see if it's you that's holding things up. You're the one who has to be willing to receive, and you're the one who needs to be obedient and put your faith in gear. Have you ever thought about the fact that answers to your prayers might hinge on your belief, your trust, your obedience, and your willingness to let God be God? Is He waiting on you?

You can look at the story in Exodus about the children of Israel on their way to the Promised Land. God provided every day for all of their needs. He was in a process with them. They had no choice but to rely on Him. He was teaching and training them because He was growing them up. They'd been slaves for 430 years in Egypt, and God needed them to listen to Him. He knew they would need to have faith in what He guided them to do without asking why. You shouldn't have the need to know why if you fully trust Him. God says that if you do it His way, He'll take you further than your way would ever get you. It's your choice. You can do it your way, or you can do it His way.

When you have a couple of days, take the time to go back and read and study about that eleven-day journey that took forty years of traveling through the desert. It begins in Exodus 13, and it's pretty lengthy. But I think you'll figure out what I'm talking about. Then ask yourself which way you'd rather go. Will it still be your way, or will you relent and go God's way. After all, God made your path, and He knows the plan He set before you. Let Him lead you. He already knows how to get there.

Don't be too busy for God and don't try to live without involving Him. He makes Himself available to you because when people are left to themselves, they do the most ridiculous things. One of those things is actually bargaining with God. Now many times these may not be people who routinely pray, but they have found themselves in serious trouble at specific times in their lives.

It reminds me of an old joke about the swimmer who goes out too far in the ocean. He tries to swim back, but the waves keep pushing against him. He begins to realize he's not going to make it to shore on his own. With each stroke he's pleading with God and promising that if God helps him make it, he'll change his life and be good forever. As he feels himself getting more tired, his promises get stronger and stronger. Toward the end his promise gets fierce, and he begins to say he'll do anything God wants him to do if He will just help him get to shore.

The irony for me is that he didn't even ask for God to save him. He only asked for God to get him to shore. Doesn't that just sound like most people? You want so badly to be out of the situation you're in that you actually begin to bargain with God. You don't really even care about what got you into trouble in the first place, you just want that quick fix. The really absurd part is that at the time you seriously think the Lord is contemplating an answer.

That story can seem comical as a joke example, but when you look at it in real life, it's kind of pitiful, isn't it? I think to God it might even be an insult, the idea that you could barter your behavior with the one who created the world. The really peculiar thing is that God would already be willing to do anything for you that you ask if you would just ask in His will and with the right heart. What He doesn't do is work on your behalf based solely on emotional outbursts of self-pity.

God has His own way of doing things, and that's in direct opposition to the way the world runs itself. The Lord tells you that if you want to be exalted high, then you have to humble yourself, and if you want to save your life, you must first lose it. Of course when He says you have to lose your life, He doesn't mean physically. He means you must give it up, give it over to Him, and let Him have control.

Not being prepared for life out in the world can be dangerous. That's what I ran into when I graduated high school and then went out into the world without a clue or even a glance ahead. Be wise and read the Bible. It explains everything.

The Christian guidelines and morals you've been teaching in your home are probably the opposite of everything your children are learning away from home. If God has a set of rules, the enemy will have opposite rules that are all designed to trick you. Be wise and clue your kids into the fact that the enemy is a counterfeit. Teach them about manipulation and promptings from the enemy, lies and deceptions, and *apples* that seem delicious but bring death.

One of the statements I've heard our older generation say is this: "If it sounds too good to be true, it probably is." I would agree to that as a general statement. Be watchful and guarded. In this age you cannot afford to let your children leave your home unprepared because that old enemy is still very much alive and moving around. If I were him, I'd begin work immediately on the sumptuous young ones just leaving home and striking out on their own. When they pack to go away to college or to leave home and go out into the world, make sure they've packed their full set of spiritual armor and their Bible.

Now there's no need to think a devil is around every corner, but it's safe to assume that you need to watch your back, be spiritually-minded, and keep the Lord by your side. Carry out your days with your mind focused on good things, and when life begins to spin, go directly to your knees.

While you're showering and getting ready for work or even while you're driving to work, pray for your day and spend some time with the Lord. If you drive alone, this would also make a great time to hear from the Lord.

Consistently survey your spiritual walk. If you begin to see changes or notice something's not right, ask the Holy Spirit to guide you, and if changes are in order, then make the changes. Don't wait. As people get older, they will tell you how they've come to know their bodies and how it acts and how they can tell when something's up. Well, you should have that same knowledge about your soul and spirit too. When you begin to feel attitudes or mood swings or you begin to become drawn to people outside of your relationship, step it up. Don't let the enemy get ahead of you.

Don't forget to praise the Lord, especially during those bad times. Sacrificial praise—that's the praise you give the Lord when you don't feel like it, when it's just hard to go there. In my opinion it's actually the best type of praise because it takes strength and determination and willpower to try.

Thanking Him throughout your day for what's occurring in your life will help to keep communication open. Having a plan for your life is also vital. If you don't know what that plan is, ask the Lord to tell you. If for some reason you haven't gotten your answer after you've been in prayer over it, then sit down and write out what you have heard from the Lord. Dwell on what the Holy Spirit keeps bringing back to your mind and anything you've gotten from your readings in the Bible. Continuing on in that forward phase will help you set some type of goal or plan for yourself.

It may be that God has something He's instructed you to do, but you haven't done it. Or it may be that you're doing something in your life you shouldn't be doing. Consequently He's holding back until you make those changes. Whatever it is, He hasn't forgotten you, so continue to seek His answer. Remember that God doesn't ignore you. He waits for you but never ignores you, and He also doesn't forget about what you pray. Until you know for sure either what He wants you to do or what His path is for you, continue on, pray, ask, and seek.

God will keep moving you into a place of higher expectations for greatness. The remarkable thing is that He not only will teach you how to attain it but will also help you to perform it. However, greatness and significance won't come unless you've surrendered and you're willing to move forward. So no matter what, no matter how many mistakes you make, it's still your faith that God honors. "Now faith is the substance of things hoped for, the evidence of things not seen" (Hebrews 11:1 KJV).

God wants your trust and knowing of Him to be solid because that's what allows faith to grow and bloom. Stay repentant, stay in belief, and continue walking out that faith. Please remember that your past doesn't cancel you out, so when the enemy comes to remind you of it, tell him to get lost in the name of Jesus.

Learn to offer up thanks to your heavenly Father and tell Him how you feel about your day and how wonderful His creations are. Just say thanks for your good moods and happy days and for protecting you and defending you. Tell Him thank you for delivering you out of bad situations and keeping stress and depression far from your mind. Begin that habit of thanking Him for everything. For the rain or the sunshine, a great movie on Saturday evening, and even the three pounds you lost. Try walking throughout your day with a sense of contentment and making continual little comments to Him. Disregard all the commotion going on around you. Don't let your emotions or your attitudes affect your situation because if you let them, they will. Put the Lord first, but let Him be the one in the center of your day.

Always trying to fix everything all by yourself doesn't work either because the Lord never intended for you to do that. He's waiting to help you, and all He wants is for you to ask. The situation doesn't have to be huge in order for you to ask for help.

God is the only one you can go to about anything and everything with no prejudice. Don't let the enemy bring to you shame or guilt, and do your best not to make excuses about your behavior. So allow the Lord to move you out of your protective and distrustful demeanor and into an optimistic and encouraging stance.

Chapter
28

To Be or Not to Be

As a woman of God, you can be such a blessing to those around you and to those not as experienced as yourself. Take it from me. You don't have to be a previous saint to help others. In fact, you don't have to be a present saint to help others. If you have a past that God is healing or has healed or you have a story of redemption, let the Lord guide you and offer that hope for something different and something good and real.

I genuinely enjoy talking with and mentoring women younger than me. They need women of faith in their lives and someone who'll tell them the truth and not leave out the uncomfortable stuff. It's my personal belief that the women of this time need to be schooled in a couple of subjects. One subject in particular comes straight out of the written Word. It's the acquiring of the taste for being amenable and open to their husbands.

It appears that education about the biblical word *submission* is sorely needed. Numerous men and women tend to believe that submission means the woman has to be subservient to her husband, who then becomes her boss. It's as if she is then relegated to becoming much like an employee. In reality, as taken from the Scriptures, the meaning of submission is actually totally the opposite of what was just mentioned.

To be submissive in your marriage means you voluntarily put yourself under the *leadership* of your husband. It's sort of like a voluntary yielding to a team effort. The both of you make up that team, and you both offer advice and ideas. Together you make your choices about whatever decisions you're contemplating. The woman ultimately sees the leadership role in her husband coming into play when a decision can't be reached because it's not unanimous. This is when the husband is permitted to make that final determination. At that point it's the husband's time to make sure he's submitted himself to God and is praying over the best choice for the both of you.

In all the reading on this subject I never came across any statement that said the husband was to be the boss. A leader guides you and will focus on the route that brings the best outcome. A boss doesn't really care about your opinion or your wants and choices.

God has put you under your husband's covering if you're married, and he is placed directly under God's covering. He's to care for you as if you were his own body, and actually I would think that places the man in a tougher position.

I went back to Genesis 3:16, where God was telling Adam and Eve and the serpent what the consequences were of their sin. Eve learned that part of hers was that her *desire* would be for her husband but that her husband would *rule* over her. It would be much like she would want him and need him and he in turn would feel power from that. When I researched the word *desire*, it brought forth a depiction that encompasses more than just the idea of longing. The entire soul and essence of the person is involved. It suggests that Eve's sense of herself, the very core of her emotionally as well as physically, will become dependent upon her husband. I can understand the hesitancy of women in their lack of want-to in this area of releasing control. But really there's no need to go there if you and your partner *both* know the truth of the word *submission*. As the woman, if the very essence of your emotional and physical needs are dependent on your husbands, wouldn't it be a wise choice to go ahead and be compliant and willing?

I cannot even tell you how many times in my own life I have wanted to take the wheel and just throw him out of the car and just go on. But if you're attempting to live out a Christian walk in your marriage, you have to do it God's way, or the travel will be very bumpy. Even though God has put this onto Eve and therefore to all women, that doesn't mean God didn't somehow work out a way of safety in your submissiveness to your Christian husband.

As a godly husband, he should lovingly interact with his wife. He should never require or ask you to do anything against God's rules. Remember—your loyalty to God is first, and with his covering over you, your husband comes directly after God. Do yourself a favor. Let your husband believe in himself and let him be the spiritual leader of the home. If you do that with the right heart, I believe he will come to you for your thoughts and wise advice. I also believe it would help to produce in him a more tender leadership. "Wives, submit yourselves to your own husbands as you do to the Lord. For the husband is the head of the wife as Christ is the head of the church, his body, of which he is the Savior" (Ephesians 5:22–23 NIV). "Husbands, love your wives, just as Christ loved the church and gave himself up for her" (Ephesians 5:25 NIV). "In this same way, husbands ought to love their wives as their own bodies. He who loves his wife loves himself" (Ephesians 5:28 NIV).

After I read those three Scriptures, I knew I would rather have the woman's role than the man's. As the husband, it appears that God has put him in the hot seat. Remember—if he's your husband, he's your covering, and he's spiritually responsible for you, his wife. This means he should be praying over you and going to the Lord in prayer over all his decisions concerning you. He also should be in prayer for decisions he makes over you two as a couple.

If you're not married, then God is your direct covering because He wants to be in the place of a husband in your life. So now you're basically inhabiting what would be the husband's spot. You'll be the one praying over your decisions concerning your life and your ministries. This time it's God who's covering you. Remember that with God in the place of your husband, you need to be submissive to Him in His leadership. Don't worry. He's the best husband you could have, and He'll always bring to you the best decision as your answer.

Chapter
29

Encounters of the More Intimate Kind

I think it's time I talked openly about another subject, namely sexual matters. If you're single—and it doesn't matter how you got that way—God has set before you some very intentional, nonflexible, strict rules about intimacy and sexual behavior. It was once my belief that God would make some allowances for me because I had been married before. I seriously didn't want to be held to the same standard as someone who had never been married. But to my dismay, as much as I wanted to believe that, I never found any proof that God could grant me my wish. This was another one of those issues that would take me a long time to figure out.

God doesn't make laws just for no reason or because He's hard to get along with. He makes them as guidelines and rules for our patterns of expected behavior. Because they're His rules and laws, if they're not followed, that becomes sin. They are not gray areas, and He doesn't tag onto them the stipulation that if you're not sure, you can disregard them. I always tried to find the gray area, but I was never successful. Believe me, God will hold you, me, and everyone else to His standard.

As a Christian woman, when you're not married to a man, God considers you to be in a marriage relationship with Him. Earlier I mentioned that I would really have a difficult time when people would tell me that very same thing. Well, now you can add me to your list of the people you thought were off the mark on this. The difference this time is that God has taught me two very special things. One is that you don't *always* have to go through something to know something. God also took the time to teach me and show me that He really could pick up that role as my husband. It was almost like that shy bride who's afraid, and her husband is forgiving in his manner and slow in his handling of her. God very patiently walked me through the entire process until that understanding in my mind and heart came together. I realized it's not some big traumatic issue. It's a love relationship that binds you with God in a trusting and confident manner. As a four-time divorced woman, God didn't hesitate to swoop in and pick me up and tuck me under His wings and protect me. He was my deliverer and my defender just as if I was a new bride. "He will cover you with his feathers, and under his wings you will find refuge; his faithfulness will be your shield and rampart. You will not fear the terror of night, nor the arrow that flies by day, nor the pestilence that stalks in the darkness, nor the plague that destroys at midday" (Psalm 91:4–6 NIV).

As your spiritual husband, God is the one caring for you and covering and protecting you, and He's there for you in every role you'll let Him. He wants for you to take that seriously, and He asks you as His marriage partner to be celibate and pure. That means being pure in the respect of not committing adultery or being otherwise sexually immoral. When you're ready to have a godly, earthly husband, He can bring him to you. But first you must die to your own self, your own desires, and self-gratification. He's not going to bring a godly prince into your life if you won't do that, and I speak to you from experience. This is one of those things the Lord patiently taught me. You have to be true to your first love and that should be God. I say first love because when you give your heart to Jesus or when you recommit your life to Jesus, your spiritual life brings you to a new beginning. Your spiritual heart is clean and fresh, and you're righteous through the blood of Christ. God should become your number-one guy. He should be first in your life, and you should always take Him with you in spirit and mind everywhere you go. Just like in your submissiveness to an earthly husband, you will need to also give God that honor. "But among you there must not be even a hint of sexual immorality, or of any kind of impurity, or of greed, because these are improper for God's holy people" (Ephesians 5:3 NIV).

Please don't let yourself down by allowing someone who enters your life to talk you into anything. Don't give away any part of your body. No matter what has occurred in your life, you're worthy of having someone who respects you. Past mistakes are gone if you've asked for forgiveness, so they do not exist. God isn't the one telling you that you're of no worth or value. It's only yourself or others who may say that or make you feel that way. God also doesn't penalize or cast you away and never allow you to have someone in your life because you're divorced. Remember that sexual immorality involves some portion of wickedness, deceit, decadence, irreverence, disloyalty, and/or indulgence. When you as a single person let desires and longings and yearnings, take you into falling prey to them, you have just entered into a very dangerous area. "Flee from sexual immorality. All other sins a person commits are outside the body, but whoever sins sexually, sins against their own body. Do you not know that your bodies are temples of the Holy Spirit, who is in you, whom you have received from God? You are not your own; you were bought at a price. Therefore honor God with your bodies" (1 Corinthians 6:18–20 NIV).

Sexual feelings and desires aren't foreign to you because they were initiated by God as physical elements of life. However, God has given clear instructions and rules about their intended purpose. When the enemy is able to get the upper hand on something you haven't protected or watched over, something you've left unrestrained, it becomes a source of weakness. It becomes that hold that's difficult to control and pulls on you constantly, causing you to debate within yourself. But these holds can and will die if you starve them, so set out to separate yourself from them.

The Bible specifies there can be no premarital sexual encounters, and because I didn't want to enter into marriage again, I felt caught. It was like a type of death sentence to my future in that area. Oh, my goodness, my mind was so mixed up. The closest thing I can compare it to is debating about whether to have cosmetic facelift surgery. You wonder if you should be wise and listen to the doctor when he explains the chances of something permanently going wrong or just go with your want. You see all the opportunities for having that youthful appearance with no wrinkles, and you get really excited. Then you look at the chances of experiencing something dreadfully wrong. These chances of wrong could include disfigurement or even death on the operating table, all for something you didn't even need. That's when you realize how big your decision just became. But you want it so badly, and your want to look young is paramount. What to do?

It becomes a huge issue because your want is so dominant and overriding. You debate and question yourself many times over, and then you decide to go ahead and satisfy that desire. What have you just done? Have you just led yourself into a death of a kind?

God does call some people to celibacy for their faithful ministry work, but I knew I was not one of them. My new Christian friend told me about God assuming that role of being my husband, but I hadn't learned it yet. I guess you can't really identify with something until it's tied into a belief. So my ignorance of what to do to keep myself from experimenting with occasional immoral acts was keeping me in a state of distress. But I desperately wanted to do it right this time, and I needed to get back to that path God had chosen for me. I didn't want to be disappointed one more time. So even though I was in my early stages of learning about correct choices, this time I actually made the right one.

My plan of attack in my own life was to capture and copy many of the Scriptures I could find on sexual immorality and read them out loud and analyze them. When I was going through my battle with fear, I had typed up Scriptures in large bold type and then taped them to the walls and doors inside my home. Psalm 91, Psalm 4:8, Proverbs 3:24, Isaiah 43:1–2, Isaiah 41:10, and 2 Timothy 1:7 were just a few of those. I did that not only for me but so the enemy would know that I meant business. It was like a warning and an alert with a physical reminder to myself of God's promised safety.

So now I had to figure out where I wanted to stand on this. I knew in my heart that if I wanted to bring peace and joy in my life, as well as my heart's desire, I had to get my act together. Was it more important to play the whining sufferer and occasionally dabble in sexual sin, or was it more important to straighten out my life? Was it also important enough to me to become who God wanted me to be, even if there was a personal cost to it? Well, because you're reading this, you know what I picked. I made my decision not to lie down and let myself be run over, or be left behind or left for dead. I wanted to be the victor this time around.

Find out what your weaknesses are. You know, go back and find out the root of them, not just the end result. Then find out what environment they thrive in and remove yourself from that environment. If watching romantic movies and seeing people kissing one another moves you into those thoughts and that desire, don't watch them. Be strong and pick up the remote and change the channel. If you were an alcoholic, you wouldn't sit at a bar and watch people drink, all the while trying to keep yourself from picking up a glass. If having a guy come over to your house and sit and watch television always develops into a make-out session, don't have him come to your home. Pick going out to the movies with him, in separate cars if necessary.

Put yourself before them. Once you make that choice to be celibate and not play around, don't give in. Make that decision. Be strong and in charge and don't waver. You'll only be able to free yourself if you remove yourself from the environment in which your weaknesses thrive. It's a matter of figuring out how much you really want that change in your life. Be that bold person, the one who figures out who they want to be, and then go for it.

While I'm typing this, I get the feeling the Holy Spirit wants to have me add something. So I want to say to you that you should never feel embarrassed or ashamed to let others know about your personal ethics, values, and morality. If you've made a decision to follow Christ and have Him in your life, then you shouldn't ever downplay or hide that. When you've decided to overcome and change, if those around you can't join that team, then they're probably going to try to fight you on it. They may be used to having you buckle under pressure, so it's natural for them to try to persuade you. Don't let others manipulate you and don't listen to the promptings that will be whispered in your ear by a source who doesn't have your best interests in mind.

God's intention for you is to be courageous. He's placed a worth inside of you, and you have to see that in order to believe in yourself. You can't allow other people to make your decisions because they're not the ones who have to live and die with them. The mere fact that you made a decision shows you're gaining in strength. So if you have to stomp your feet, scream into a pillow, and have a hysterical breakdown, do it and then get back up. When you've gotten yourself together again, hold your head up, smile, thank Jesus, and congratulate yourself for being strong and working through it.

You know I've come a long way, and I don't do all the same harmful things I used to. But that doesn't mean my mind or my memory has been erased. I can still put together all the pieces of the games that get played and the things that go through your mind when I'm confronted with sexual situations. I've personally used every excuse in the book to attempt to withdraw from being the guilty party, in this area of my life.

This time, when confronted with an opportunity to engage in a sexual situation, you feel as if you know how to handle it. You've gained more information and received more of God's teaching, so it should work. You've gone through all the scenarios and found your root of the problem and have realized what triggers you in your environment. You've spent a lot of mental and emotional time trying to work it out. You really don't want to find yourself in that precarious place again. I would venture to say that the whole time you've been doing that, subconsciously you've set yourself up with an alibi or a way out of taking the blame in case you fumble. That's because you know in your gut it may not work for you, and you don't want to fail again. In fact, you probably can't stomach the thought.

Your vision is clouded in this area, and once you've gotten yourself into thinking negatively, your mind begins to work overtime.

You don't want to dabble because you know it's wrong, but you already know there may be a chance you'll blow it. It's messy at best, and normally all the thoughts that come to you are perceived subconsciously. Your brain will tell you that the guy is right there with you, doing the same thing you are, so he's just as responsible. Then that prompting from the enemy says to you that he's the man and that he should be the stronger one. It's absolutely shameful. I know you won't do it on purpose, and I know that because I've been through it. Even though you've mentally played the blame game, you'll still feel shame, and you just can't fathom the thought of being guilty and failing one more time. So do it the right way in the beginning. If you're serious, pull in God to walk with you through this. He's capable of delivering you from anything. When you're trying to overcome something involving addictions or strongholds by yourself, you can just figure that your success rate will be around … uh, let's say zero.

Don't be embarrassed to include God. He's the one who thought up the idea of sexual participation, and He's the one who developed and created it. It's no secret to Him He knows everything, so there's no reason to hide.

In my estimation sexual sin may be one of the hardest to overcome. It's like being on a diet. It's rough. Food is a necessity, so when your body needs it, your belly rumbles. But when you have a craving or a particular want for a special food, your memory of how good it was and how delicious it smelled and looked gets involved. The diet part comes into play when you have to figure out what you can have and what you can't have. It's the same with sexual desires. It's a part of what God gave you internally, but you have to put yourself on that sexual sin diet. If you've prayed and studied the Word and heard ministers speak about this, you know you cannot go there. But you and I both know forbidden fruit looks yummy, but it brings with it a death of a kind.

First Corinthians 6:18 tells you God wants you to flee or run away from sexual immorality. He says all other sins you commit are sins outside the body, but when you sin sexually, that's a sin against your own body. Once you became a believer and follower of Christ, you received the Holy Spirit, and He resides within you. You don't belong to yourself anymore because Jesus paid for you with His life. So God expects you to honor Him with your body, not sin against it. That may be why this is such an area of interest to the enemy. It not only involves a want for the taste of immorality, but it hinders you in your relationship with the Holy Spirit. When you choose to sin, you'll typically separate yourself and back away a little because of the guilt. "Do you not know that your body is a temple of the Holy Spirit, who is in you, whom you have received from God? You are not your own" (1 Corinthians 6:19 NIV).

Look for boundaries, for those lines to be drawn to keep your behavior contained. Build them into your performance. Don't cross them and don't let others cross them. Draw a line as to what's acceptable and what isn't and tell others your boundary guidelines. Then don't give in to them. So if you're single, that boundary line regarding sexual activity should be straight and bold. If your boyfriend or fiancée is a Christian and he really cares for you, he'll want to keep you safe, and that's how you should feel about him.

Think about how many people and how many times you've let other people walk right over your boundaries at your own personal and spiritual expense. Maybe that was because they didn't know about your boundaries. Be loud and clear about your own personal rules, and don't let others attempt to guilt you into behaving differently than you know you should as a Christian. If you let someone else talk you into something, they won't take the consequence of your action. You will. Even if the person is guilty as well, you'll each reap your own distinct consequence.

So begin by drawing your boundaries with small lines. Don't pull too many subjects together. For example, don't make sex one long boundary line. Separate it out a little but still be exact. Take each of them individually and remember that if your border lines get too long, failure becomes too easy because there's so much wiggle room. Sometimes divorce can be the result of not having any built-in boundaries around single subjects. You need definite preset boundary lines for items such as finances, savings, in-laws, tithing, entertainment, corrective behavior for the kids, etc.

Drawing those boundary lines will help the married and the single. Matthew 5:28 says that anyone who looks upon another lustfully has already committed adultery with them in their hearts. Well, that's a pretty solid statement. That should leave no questions as to what God expects and where your boundary line should be regarding adultery. I don't believe you could ever convince me that it's possible to have any type of physical togetherness without eventually thinking about or wanting it to go further. Generally holding hands will lead to eventual embraces, and that leads to kisses and so on and so on. Let's face it. You're human. This is tough and something I wasn't ever before able to permanently conquer on my own. But when God revealed to me that He was not going to bring to me a godly man until I could figure that out and be in absolute and determined control, I chose to put God on my team and get that one settled.

God doesn't want His godly men tempted and blamed and put into situations they shouldn't be in. Don't think He will give you His best before you're ready to treat them the way they should be treated. If God's willing to do that for them, He's certainly willing to do that for you. Makes sense, doesn't it?

So now you know your victory over your desires has to be attended to with painful effort. Everything bestowed on you by God was intended to help save you from your sins, not to put you into them. Don't let your natural senses keep you continually committing transgressions by your lack of caution and failure to hold to your boundary line. Don't lead others into temptation, like you do when you leave it up to them to stop the behavior. Provide your own barriers and boundaries and stick to them. Don't tempt men by wearing low-cut blouses or really high skirts because what you're really doing is setting them up for what Matthew 5 talks about. Purposefully leading a man to commit a sin by lusting makes you a partner in that sin, and it's wrong. Sometimes there's a fine line between being that good-looking, beautifully dressed woman and being that woman who has gone overboard in her sexiness. Find your lines, find your boundaries, and don't cross them for yourself or for anyone else. Don't let yourself talk yourself into things you know will damage what you're trying to accomplish.

I remember thinking I was okay because it was so rare that I let myself cross my inadequate boundaries. I believed God knew I really didn't want to go there, but I just didn't know how to resist. I assumed somehow He would know I couldn't possibly be at fault. Dangerous, it's very dangerous to allow yourself to sin against your own body and then make excuses for it.

Deep inside I knew it was wrong; however, it was true that I'd had no teaching on the hows and how-nots. When it says to flee from sexual immorality, that's exactly what it means. Run for your life and discard it from your thinking. Don't allow it to roam around inside your head and continually try to control your thoughts. There are so many things tied to sexual sin that it's really dangerous to leave your mind open to the possibilities. If the enemy can find one boundary line that has a possible opening in that area, he'll blow right through it.

Let the Holy Spirit prompt you and give you insight into how to deal with it. As a caution, I can tell you that if you don't tell the enemy to stop and get out in the name of Jesus, he'll continue and then continue some more. He wants to win this battle because it involves your character and the integrity of you and your Christian standards. But just like any other sin, God expects you to separate out or weed out what isn't morally correct and what isn't His standard. Maybe a better way to state that would be to have a definite mind-set of what God's rules and parameters are, and once you know, you can resolve yourself not to stray and give in. If you can't do that, admit to the Lord that you're having trouble and you really need His help. The biggest help you can give yourself is to be certain of your desire to stop playing around with your eternity. God doesn't give you rules because He's a strict daddy. He gives you rules for the purposes involving your life path, your future, your eternity, and those whose lives you touch. So get big in God, be strong, and cast those imaginations down and always try to remember what faction is behind it. Is it sinful and evil, or is it godly and right?

Don't give in because you're worth more than that. Don't give yourself away through sexual means or by making short-term decisions that you haven't prayed about. When I occasionally would let myself become involved, I came away feeling unworthy, full of blame and guilt, not trustable. I know listening to your man tell you he loves you and knowing you love him, encourages your flesh to assume God will overlook what's happening. He won't. Now you've just become a party to compromise. You may think that because you've committed yourself verbally to each other or because you've received a ring, you feel as if that's a marriage, one done without the legal papers. Are you willing to risk your eternity on that? Are you willing to risk your relationship with your heavenly Father over sex?

God has taught me that I was giving myself away very cheaply. I was willing to compromise on true love, truth, and honesty just for someone saying he loved me. But when you're willing to compromise, how committed is that other person? How dedicated will that person be to you? How concerned over your life and your happiness will he be? How much contentment do you think you will really receive from this?

I personally don't want to give any more of my life over to what I know in my heart is wrong or even questionable. I want to do it God's way because it's wildly refreshing and rewarding. I feel clean and washed and ready for whatever God brings my way. God can become the love of your life, and His love for you is unwavering. Your chances of getting everything that is best for you is 100 percent!

So set your boundaries and know that God is your only path. After all, it's only sex. Oh, come on now, quit rolling your eyes. It really is only great for a very small portion of time, and then it's totally gone. But you have to live with the burden of what you just did. The really horrible thing is that because it's a fleshly sin, having a sexual encounter only encourages your need for it to happen again.

You can't expect your sin to be forgiven when you walk up to God and say, "I'm sorry. Please forgive me," knowing you're going to do it again. You may not want it to happen again; however, if you don't put change in the mix, it will, and inside you know that. God says repentance is doing your best to never do it again and begin to have a change of mind and heart. Following Jesus and wanting to be more like Him will draw you to that. Pray, pray, and pray.

For single people, sex is not the doorway to a cherishing and adoring love. Sex won't automatically bring happiness. Sex will not fill that place in your heart that begs for someone to love you. Sex won't make you feel valuable and worthy, and sex doesn't automatically make that partner feel forever bonded with you.

So when you're trying to be free, tell that old devil to get lost. You aren't bound to him. He only wants you to think that. Don't let your fleshly mind override your good spiritual senses. Put yourself in check and make a verbal demand that your thoughts be pure and moral and within God's boundaries. Get *big* in God. Be determined and not weak. Through Jesus Christ and His blood sacrifice, you have become worthy and valuable. Don't think that because you had a past, this makes you no good because that is not at all how the Lord sees it.

Be humble, gentle, and compliant, and let the Lord love you with everything He has to give you. I promise you that you won't feel a lack of anything. There won't be voids and gaps of any type in your life because His love is so encompassing that it covers everything. You won't have years of crying every night because you're desperately hungry for someone to just love you. You won't feel that sad and empty feeling when you show up once again at a function by yourself. You won't have that mad desire for sex or a yearning and longing for someone to hold you and show you he cares. When those thoughts come over you, they'll be easier to put down because of that marital relationship between you and God. Your Creator will love you forever and treat you as no person on earth could. Even if you're physically married, the Lord is still there for you the same as anyone else. He's got you totally covered, and His arms are always available for spiritual hugs. Thoughts will come because the enemy is mean, but they'll be controllable. Make your mind up to be who you want to be inside. Don't let anyone else deter you from your peace.

I craved intimacy and hungered for companionship, but those emotions no longer visit me, at least not with strength and depth. For the first time in my adult life, while I'm on my own, I'm not lonely. How can I be lonely when God is always with me? How can I be lonely when He's available to me every moment of my day and night forever? How can I be lonely when He's given me such complete rest, unconditional love, attachment without hidden strings, and a love with no requirements? How can I be lonely with a relationship that isn't filled with ugly things and offers a peace beyond all else? I know He's going to protect me and defend me until I die and begin my eternity with Him. When I reach heaven, I'll never have to deal with any of the enemy's ugly threats and attempts to change my life or bring in sadness. But while I'm on the earth, my God will cover me with His wings and protect me and defend me and stand in back of me, to the side of me, and in front of me, in defense against all opposition.

Chapter
30

Strength in the Journey

Throughout this journey God maintained a process of helping me wade through all the bits and pieces of a disjointed life. God was very gentle, as I felt a pulling away and a discarding of layers of discontent, lack of understanding, and constant inability to be hopeful for change. At some point He began to unveil an awareness of a true ministry and the calling He'd placed within my life. As a bonus, I began to recognize no matter how unhappy and bleak my life appeared to me, God had never left my side. He hadn't left me when I forgot to pay attention to Him. Nor had He left me during those times when I didn't want to listen to what He had to say. He was proving to me that He was constant and I could trust Him to never leave me or forsake me. I was beginning to fully comprehend that God has never backed off. I knew that He wasn't going to move on to someone else who paid more attention to Him. He continually demonstrated to me that He would never be the one in my life who said one thing and then did another. I know now without a doubt my God is true to His Word. He's honest and not corrupt, guiltless and not guilty, truthful and not a liar. He's perfect.

As a believer and follower of Jesus, you can count on the fact that His love for you is not only unconditional but also unrelenting and unfaltering. Thank goodness the Father's treatment and handling of you isn't based on your love and dedication to Him. It's based on how much He loves you.

Everyone was made in His image, and everyone's spirit is eternal. That was His plan all along. However, it wasn't His will that man should sin and therefore be separated from their Creator and have to one day die. He wants for you to love Him and recognize the salvation available to you because He wants you to be with Him forever.

When Adam and Eve sinned, it changed everything and brought into the world a different pattern of expectation between man and their Creator. Their sin initiated an actual separation, and they couldn't any longer enjoy walking and talking with the Lord during the day as they had before. Sin had surrounded them. Habakkuk 1:13 says God can't look upon wickedness because His eyes are too pure to behold evil. So there was really no way for man to undo what He'd done. Christ stepped up and volunteered to give Himself as the ultimate sacrifice on the cross. It meant He had to leave heaven in order to be birthed and become the sacrificial Lamb. Christ's sacrifice for you is the only reason that separation is gone. God can now look at you through the blood covering of Christ's righteousness. You would never be righteous on your own. You couldn't ask for it, and you could never earn it. This unique and developing relationship enables you to be in constant fellowship with the Lord. You don't have to go through anyone else or get an appointment. He's just always there. He always has time, and He'll never rush you. The Lord is the one who brings freedom from the stress and pressures of life because of His willingness to take all our burdens.

As you come before the Lord in prayer, He strengthens your spiritual heart, calms your fears, and lifts you up. His power loosens those holds and bands from around your neck and trades you the garment of praise for your old spirit of heaviness.

> And provide for those who grieve in Zion—to bestow
> on them a crown of beauty instead of ashes, the oil
> of joy instead of mourning, and a garment of praise
> instead of a spirit of despair. They will be called oaks
> of righteousness, a planting of the LORD for the
> display of his splendor.
>
> —Isaiah 61:3 NIV

Chapter

31

Faith

When people give their hearts to Christ and are saved, it's usually based on a recent experience or a newfound discovery of Him. That first love grows into adoration and worship and brings forward a relationship between you and God that becomes an intimate spiritual connection. "For I say, through the grace given unto me, to every man that is among you, not to think of himself more highly than he ought to think; but to think soberly, according as God hath dealt to every man the measure of faith" (Romans 12:3 KJV).

Scripture tells us that God provided everyone with the measure of faith. It's not *a* measure of faith. It's *the* measure, meaning God allowed for everyone to have the same portion available to them. If God had been using a teaspoon to dole out faith, everyone would have exactly a teaspoon. This definitely shows you it's not determined by quantity. It's determined by the quality and depth of use and belief. Some people never exercise their faith or even believe it's really in them, but that doesn't make it any less truth.

Matthew 17:19–21 speaks about the mustard seed as the model for how little faith it would take to move a mountain. I realized

I'd heard a lot of talk about the mustard seed, but I'd never looked at one, so I went online and checked it out. The seed is very tiny, and in the pictures shown, they're likened to the tip of a pencil; however, some grow to be very large plants. Maybe this is one of the points Christ was trying to make. It's a reference for using the smallest amount to get back the biggest return. "And without faith it is impossible to please God, because anyone who comes to him must believe that he exists and that he rewards those who earnestly seek him" (Hebrews 11:6 NIV).

I could never be convinced that the Lord would have said that you couldn't please Him without faith, unless He had given full provision for you to have that faith. Faith is about right belief in the power and authority available and then the ability to develop the measure provided. To work toward developing a depth of faith or heightened intensity, your thought process, your actions, and your strength of character will all get involved.

The more I learned about God and who He is, the more I hungered for truth about Him. I wanted to know everything. I wanted to understand what I felt I had been missing, especially when I was dealing with personal healings of the physical body.

So I decided to put it together much like an easy outline, something I could refer back to. I discovered my framework of faith was like a balance beam, much like that used in a sporting event. Faith itself would be the primary source or the base of your relationship with the Lord, the solid piece to stand on. Because of the surety of the base, you'd be able to stand upright and hold your footing before taking a next step. But because of the need for you to be "exacting" in that faith walk, so you wouldn't fall, you would have to know your steps ahead of time.

My first step in my walk of faith is trust. For me trust had to come first because without it I wouldn't take that next step because I'd be too uncertain. It's a trust that says you know what God intends for you is always the best. It's also a trust that allows you to believe His love for you is so completely remarkable that He would never lead you astray. It's allowing yourself to accept that if He promises something, you can take Him at His Word, and it's a conviction of the validity of His commitment to you.

My second step would be belief. This belief is a confidence and a certainty that the Father in heaven, the Creator of the universe, is the ultimate power He says He is. It's a well-grounded assurance of that for which you hope and a conviction of what you can't see in the physical realm. It's the act of not thinking about it, not mulling it over, and not doing some kind of self-examination, but a right belief, the kind God requires without evidence. A belief that says I don't just believe in God but I actually believe God, belief that allows yourself to just go with it, accepting that it is the absolute truth.

For the third step on the balance beam, I refer to loyalty. It's your constant, faithful, and persistent devotion and commitment to what you have trusted and believed to be true. It's the part you don't let go of, but rather you hold on to it and boldly exercise your righteousness through Christ.

The fourth and last basic step is a knowing. The word *knowing* means to have a deliberate, perceptive, significant, and conscious awareness. You can know that your God is God. You can know that He is deity. You can know that He is the I AM, encompassing all and everything. You can know that He will be anything and everything you need Him to be. That knowing allows you to be bold in asking for your wants, needs, and desires. It's a knowing that Jesus took everything you deserved, and now you're being gifted with everything Jesus deserves. "For the eyes of the LORD range throughout the earth to strengthen those whose hearts are fully committed to him" (2 Chronicles 16:9 NIV).

First Corinthians 10:13 says God will provide to you a way of escape from what you get yourself into. I totally believe He's your safety, and you can ask for and expect protection. For me, these steps were the only way I could make it through those dark nights when fear would have normally taken my peace. It was new to me then, and I walked that balance beam carefully. But now I know the steps, and I know the truth. I have that knowing, that He is who He said He is and that I can have total and unrestrained trust and faith.

If you've asked the Lord for an answer to a prayer or maybe for a healing and you've seen nothing in your life change, then you'll probably think nothing has happened. Doubt may set in, and when that takes place, your mind begins to accept worry, skepticism, and uncertainty. It opens up the avenue of listening to negativity from not only the enemy but also well-doers. Don't go there. Go back to the basic steps and get sure-footed again.

Sometimes in the beginning of my new walk with the Lord, even during my actual prayer I would begin to let my mind wonder. As I said the words, I'd question if I was asking too much or if I was too presumptuous in thinking God would allow me to have my answer. You may even think that God hasn't heard you or that He's too busy or you just don't have that coming to you. But don't let that thinking command the situation. When you doubt, it's as if you've just erased all the faith that you brought into the situation. Doubt and worry cause a lack of faith, so don't go there. Don't lose any precious ground you've gained in your walk of faith. The very moment you prayed and made that request, God heard it. Remember He can do all things for all of His children all at the same time.

Matthew 14:28–29 provides a description of a time when the disciples were in their boat on the lake. It says the boat was being tossed around by the wind and waves. That's when they saw someone walking on the water, and it scared them. Jesus called out and said He was the one on the water. Peter asked Jesus to confirm if it was indeed Him. Jesus answered back and then Peter stepped out of the boat and walked on the water to meet Him. As he stood on the water, he then saw the wind and became afraid and he started to sink.

Peter was witnessing a miracle and knew in His heart that it was Jesus he was walking toward. He was so concentrated on his Lord that I'm not sure he'd really figured out what he was actually doing. But when he took his eyes off Jesus, he began to doubt and became afraid. That's when he began to sink, but Jesus was there to catch him.

Simply put, Peter had enough faith to get himself out of the boat and onto the water, but his faith wasn't strong enough for him to stand up in the storm. He was in the middle of a miracle, but he couldn't finish it because he allowed fear to overcome him. He should never have taken his eyes off Jesus because then all he could see was surrounding trouble. He should have focused his eyes only on what he knew to be true. "He gives strength to the weary and increases the power of the weak. Even youths grow tired and weary, and young men stumble and fall; but those who hope in the LORD will renew their strength. They will soar on wings like eagles; they will run and not grow weary, they will walk and not be faint" (Isaiah 40:29–31 NIV).

James 1:7–8 speaks about being double-minded. It says that if you are unstable in your ways you should not think that God would give you anything. I'd heard people refer to being double-minded, many times, but I'd always felt there must be more tied into the meaning.

So I began reading from the beginning of the chapter. The first four words of Verse 2, tell you to *consider it pure joy* when you face trials of many kinds. It indicates that those trials are what will test your faith. I wondered about the choice of those four words in that verse and I wanted to understand why they in particular, were chosen.

The first word to catch my eye was the word *consider*. I had never before paid attention to it when reading that verse. It took me a while to understand that there were actually two different ways to view your trials. Because you have a choice as to how to view them, you would now have to consider, which of those ways to go.

When a trial hits you in the face, normally your first choice is to just *react*. This reaction will happen immediately. But a second way of looking at your trial would be to *respond* and not just to *react*. Responding could mean that when presented with the trial, you've taken time to stop and pray and ask for God's counsel. When considering your choices you will either take God out of the situation or you will put Him in charge.

The other word I questioned was the word *joy*. Why would I ever in the normal realm of things, believe that I should be joyful for difficult circumstances and trials? When I began to read more about how the words, happiness and joy, were represented in the New Testament, in their original language, I began to have more understanding.

Happiness was generally a word used to express feelings about external or outer circumstances. However, joy was a word used to express inner contentment in spite of the external circumstances. That's a big difference.

When your situations don't go the way you want and don't make you happy, through God's grace you can still experience a peace. When you allow God to be in control and don't question Him, you won't have to live on that emotional roller coaster because you'll know He's in control.

As I continued reading, I realized I was about to be taught some very strong truths that I knew I needed to have. I was about to discover a reason for the testing.

The Scripture says your trials will bring testing which then will develop perseverance. Then that perseverance, or what might be thought of as an unwavering resolve, or a determination, has to finish its work to bring forward maturity and completeness. You joyfully carry on as you walk your way through the entire trial, maintaining your faith, continuing to be strong, and remaining unshakable.

The verse goes on to say that if anyone lacks wisdom, they should ask the Lord for it with belief and without doubt. I read that sentence over several times but I just wasn't sure I had a full understanding of the concept of the word *wisdom,* when used in that verse. So I decided to dig in and study. I began to grasp the concept that asking for wisdom would mean you have a desire to understand how to endure your trials with joy. It was as if the Lord was saying that this godly wisdom would help you understand how to navigate through your storm and still remain joyful. Once learned, this would promote living peacefully, yet obediently, before God in the midst of chaos.

God doesn't want you to question Him about why He does things the way He does. Just know that it's His desire for you to grow and gain strength from the trials that come from your circumstances. Ask Him to help you accept His best for you. Like it or not, you live on earth and you will have trials. These trials provide Christians with a way of standing in faith and letting God develop you and increase your spiritual maturity and trust. "I have told you these things, so that in me you may have peace. In this world you will have trouble. But take heart! I have overcome the world" (John 16:33 NIV).

219

James 1:6 goes on to say that doubt is like a wave of the sea, blown and tossed about by the wind. If you doubt and question God, you won't receive anything from Him and you won't have learned from the trial. Did you catch that? It said you won't receive anything from the Lord. It will have been a trial without benefit.

When you doubt, it means you have uncertainty and maybe a lack of confidence in the knowing. All of those can lead to distrust and unbelief. If left unattended, they will become a separation between you and God. At that point I would say, you're not in a secure place.

Mark 9:23 says everything is possible to those who believe. So when you pray and ask for something, be clear and precise. Don't pray in a confusing manner. Know God's promises and understand what He's taught you through your trials. When you petition the Lord, don't hesitate, don't doubt, don't question, and don't be fearful. Allow Him the discretion of being God and don't put conditions on Him or tell Him how to answer you.

Learn your steps and use them to strengthen your faith and your walk with the Lord. Remember—your measure of faith is already built inside of you. When you've got that in your heart and mind, that's when it all opens up, and your understanding of what's involved is seen with your spiritual eyes.

When you come before the Lord and petition Him to perform a miracle in your life, it means you are prepared to stand with your armor on. Not wavering, not being doubled-minded, and not just hoping and wishing. Visualize that miracle in your mind's eye, believe and begin to walk in faith toward it. Keep your mind strong and don't worry.

Put yourself on that balance beam and use those faith steps to bring you to the end. Stand in victory to defend what God has already set in place for you. Don't try to fight the battle yourself because that's not the position God has set for you. "Therefore put on the full armor of God, so that when the day of evil comes, you may be able to stand your ground, and after you have done everything, to stand" (Ephesians 6:13 NIV).

Once you pray, continue standing in faith, leaving it to God. You can be done with self-effort because you know God will take on the battle and bring you His answer. Don't continue to worry what more you need to do to bring about your miracle. If you labor in your attempt at faith, it becomes a *work* instead of an occurrence of His grace. When you pray, trust God for the answer. He doesn't need your help, but He does want your faith. You've prayed. You've trusted. You've believed. You've stayed loyal. You've worn your full armor, and now you're standing with all of that, knowing Him, your God. Don't forget to give Him thanks for being there for you and with you. Thank Him in advance for bringing to you His answer. You're doing what He's asked. Resting in that releases you from anxiety, worry, and uncertainty. Now continue to stand fully clad in your armor, waiting expectantly in anticipation.

Chapter

32

A Little Light on the Subject

This is the message we have heard from him and declare
to you: God is light; in him there is no darkness at all.
If we claim to have fellowship with him and yet walk
in the darkness, we lie and do not live out the truth.

—1 John 1:5–6 NIV

When Jesus spoke again to the people, he said, "I am
the light of the world. Whoever follows me will never
walk in darkness, but will have the light of life."

—John 8:12 NIV

This first Scripture indicates that God is light, and with Him all is
opened. Nothing is hidden, and truth is revealed. The devil—or
the enemy as I like to call him—is darkness or the absence of truth,
which is exactly the opposite of God.

The second Scripture indicates that Jesus is the light in the world
in which we live. As long as you follow Him, you will never have to
be in darkness or ignorance of truth again.

Maybe it's a lot like when you have *the* measure of faith. That measure is given by God, but by exercising that faith, it grows in strength and stature. Your light from Christ will be the same. It'll blossom outward as you take on wisdom and will grow in intensity while you develop and surrender to what you've been taught.

Light, or knowledge and truth, keeps you on the straight path, helps in your warfare, helps to keep sin at bay, helps to recognize the enemy and to encourage your faith. Light will prove your trust and belief in the Lord has been correct. "Truly I tell you, if anyone says to this mountain, 'Go, throw yourself into the sea,' and does not doubt in their heart but believes that what they say will happen, it will be done for them" (Mark 11:23 NIV).

I had always thought speaking to a mountain and expecting it to listen and obey was a really big commitment to faith and a large expectation. Because of its massive connection to failure or success, I felt there had to be more to it than just what that verse indicated. I assumed the Lord must have had hidden goodies tied up inside because of the matter-of-fact way it was stated; however, I had no idea if that was really true.

One morning while I was listening to my pastor speak on this very Scripture, my mind was immediately opened to a new revelation. I began to get a mental view of that mountain, and it looked different than I thought it would. This one looked familiar. It looked like it was made up of my stuff, the bundle of junk I'd always carried around but much bigger. It was full of sorrow, defeat, insecurity, failure, lies, and trickery. Then I realized I'd been right about that Scripture holding much more in it than just a literal mountain because it just became very personal to me.

In that simply stated verse given in Mark 11:23, Jesus is offering to you real truth. I viewed it as if He was telling me that even those things that appeared gigantic and mountainous and seemed overwhelming weren't. It's as if they are of no real consequence even though they appear as mountains. When you speak to them through your faith and belief in what God's told you and the authority of Jesus, they're subject to that authority, and they have to obey.

The ease in which this verse is given is significant, and the resulting victory is just as significant. It's not supposed to be something you have to work at, and that was such a big lesson for me. It's done through your confidence in your faith, your authority, which is given to you by Jesus, your belief in God, and what He says you can have. The Lord doesn't want you to be overwhelmed or burdened, and that's why He gave you *the* measure of faith and the use of His authority. Remember when I talked about dating guys who had confidence and how I could borrow their confidence when we were together? Well, just as I finished writing this last sentence about authority, the Lord reminded me of that. Because I don't have any spiritual authority on my own, Jesus gave me His with His full permission to use it. It's like He's telling me, "Go ahead, child. You have a right to tell that mountain to go. It doesn't have a choice. It has to obey because you're speaking through My authority combined with your faith and belief. It doesn't have a chance. Tell it to go."

In thinking about the light and the truth, it's just like what the Holy Spirit revealed to me that Sunday while I was listening to my pastor. I'd received a personal, instantaneous insight into the meaning of what that mountain represented. Without the Lord showing me His light, I could have read that verse forever without knowing the full meaning God had for me. "Then you will know the truth, and the truth will set you free" (John 8:32 NIV).

Develop your relationship with the Lord and let Him show you the truth of everything He has for you. Hold that tightly unto your spirit heart or what I like to call your *knower*. Once you've gained that light and truth in your knower, and you know, that you know, that you know, it will always be there. Even the enemy can't take it away from you and he will never again successfully work in that area of your life. Do yourself a favor and don't be complacent or ignorant of truthfulness. Become enlightened with the Word, covering your bases over all topics, subjects, and questions.

Since my revelation about how little faith it takes to move mountains in your life, the Lord has opened to me a new arena of thinking. He's widened my sphere of possibilities, showing me not only what changes can happen in my life but also what I can in turn bring to others.

As a follower of Christ, He will always be there for you, guiding and directing you out of dark places. For me it was a breathtaking revelation when I recognized Jesus wasn't leaving me in the dark. You know, that place I was always fearful of, the place where the enemy works. God had made for me a provision even before He had made me. As long as I pursued Him and surrendered to Him, I would be in the light, and He would be right beside me.

Now you know that any amount of light dispels darkness, so that automatically means that darkness is not equal in power to light. Knowing the enemy *is* the darkness means he does not have even close to the same characteristics or power that God holds. Now as a believer, everything you face in your life will necessitate a choice and subsequent decision. How you respond to those decisions is more than just important. When circumstances turn into a crisis, be careful not to let doubt chip away at your faithful foundation. When you doubt, you're actually saying you don't trust God to fulfill His promises outlined in the Word. Your base of faith and trust in Him is vital, and it's what holds everything upright. It's the only way.

So stand tall and firm in your faith and don't give away ground you can't afford to give. The manifestation of your goal depends on holding on to hope and walking and talking faith through your problem. "For our struggle is not against flesh and blood, but against the rulers, against the authorities, against the powers of this dark world and against the spiritual forces of evil in the heavenly realms" (Ephesians 6:12 NIV).

All along the travels the Lord was walking with me, my love for Him was growing, and my faith was becoming stronger. I am totally convinced that God is exactly who He says He is, and I believe absolutely that if He says He will do it, He will do it.

I believe God created everything, including the entire universe, including mankind and angels. I believe the written Word of God, the Bible, is exactly how He wants it to be. I cannot even begin to consider that my God would send His Word, His truth, His light out into the world for all to read and hear and not have it exactly as He wants it. Remember Jesus *is* the Word. So even though it was written down by man, it was definitely inspired by God, and He acted as the spiritual editor and publisher.

I am the Alpha and the Omega, the First and the Last,
the Beginning and the End.
—Revelation 22:13 NIV

Chapter

33

Abuse

In our society there's been such a breakdown of moral and spiritual teachings, and our belief of God has been so devalued that our families are suffering. It appears that many homes are just not that safe haven they need to be.

It was only a couple of years ago that I led my first Bible Study for women, and one of the lessons in the study was about abuse. I asked my class of thirteen women if any of them believed they had incurred physical or emotional abuse or had been raped or made to endure molestation or incest. Eleven ladies out of thirteen raised their hands. I literally felt as if my heart had just broken for them, and I had never conceived of a total that high. Well, just the other day one of the leaders of a different women's group in another town said she posed this same question to the women attending her group. Her total was a staggering 100 percent. Please don't be misguided into thinking these situations haven't happened or are currently not happening to the Christian women who surround you.

It's heartbreaking when you find a true victim who doesn't see herself as the victim but as the perpetrator. I think this might happen because she's been told time and time again that she deserves what's happening, because she herself has caused the situation. I've been through this process and remember being told it was my fault and I only had myself to blame for the results. When you're involved with someone like this, you begin to believe what's being said. You're left with the heartbreak of knowing that if you hadn't been so lacking, or so stupid, or if you had been more like the woman he wanted, he wouldn't have had to treat you that way.

Every day women walk about in their daily lives, believing they're at fault and deserving of the abuse being inflicted on them. This seems to be especially true if the offender was someone who didn't display this type of behavior prior to a marriage. Often embarrassment accompanies humiliation and disgrace when the victim doesn't incur actual physical marks or end up at the hospital. Many believe no one will understand that relentless and unceasing neglect, screaming, exploitation, cruelty, character assassination, incessant insults, fighting and yelling with foul language, and never-ending criticisms are types of emotional abuse. Of course, there are also the many physical types as well.

If you're married to someone who constantly tells you in no uncertain words that you are not what or who he wants and you never will be, you have an unbelievably hard way to live. It seems this person enjoys telling you that you'll never be good enough, and he resents the fact that you're in his life. Then he smiles and appears to take great delight in letting you know he must have been crazy to have chosen you. Those are mind-numbing and confidence-shredding words being fed into your soul. These offenders drill and drill and drill into your head that you're responsible for every conceivable and imaginable fault.

However, it's my opinion that the offender isn't really trying to correct any problem. He just wants you to believe what he's saying. Not only does he desire for you to feel horrible and feel unworthy, but he may also go to great lengths to accomplish just that. These people want you to have to depend on them and let them control you. My guess is that these are some seriously angry people and possibly haters of women. They believe making you the guilty party automatically puts them in the clear for anything wrong they do. If they can make you mentally accept that guilt, then that means your guilt is real and their guilt ceases to exist. It enables them in their schemes and in their twisted thinking to continue their controlling abuse, pattern of misbehavior, and marital affairs.

I've been a party to a marriage relationship where the male had a severe anger and control problem. When others were present, he would take opportunities to demean or embarrass her, and then he would grin as he watched to see how she reacted. In my opinion his actions led me to believe he was a coward. He wasn't bold enough to go ahead and make a statement to the world that he was an abuser. He instead chose to torment her.

Abuse victims may survive physically, but there's always a sideline casualty, and one of the biggest is the death of trust. When it's a spouse who violates your trust, you struggle with self-worth because you wonder why, and you feel as if you must be the reason. Many times new young wives have a loyalty to their husbands, and with that in mind, they let their husbands become their guides and trainers in this new life. When the person you're learning from chooses to violate your trust, you come away hurt and empty. It's not just losing the trust you had for that person or relationship. It's the fact that you've lost the ability to trust anyone, especially a man.

One result of abuse can be the victim's consistent need for affirmation or approval, and this was my specialty. I desperately looked for some type of approval from someone. That you, inside of you, needs the encouragement and affirmation, to offer some reason why you still matter. Of course, this varies depending on the types of abuse and types of offenders, but I think this is a reality for the majority of cases with people I've known.

Another consequence may be the shame that becomes part of your life. You may feel ashamed because you chose to marry someone without knowing he had abusive tendencies. Or you may feel ashamed because of a rape or molestation or incidents of incest. Or it could just be that you personally didn't feel shame, but the offender put that on you and made you wear it. If the situation goes on long enough, the shame you've put on, regardless of who put it on you, will become your daily garment, and you will assume ownership.

What I really want to say to you is that when you have guilt, that's a feeling that you've done something wrong. Shame is the feeling that you are the something that is wrong. It's like wearing a shroud over you that says there's something wrong with me. That feeling may inhabit every decision you make, and you'll only be capable of seeing yourself as unworthy. Please don't let disgrace and humiliation encapsulate your life. Please don't ever assume that because you've done something wrong or made a wrong decision in your past, this makes you a bad person.

Yes, you may do wrong things, but as a believer, nothing is capable of making you a wrong person. You're made in the image of God, and that person inside of your spirit is exactly who He wants you to be. That shroud isn't even real, and those bumps and bruises and voids still left in your life don't change the real you that God formed in the womb. He gives to you His unconditional love even though as sinful humans, it's not something deserved. He has put no restrictions or conditions on His love for you because His love is the same yesterday, today, and forever just as He is the same yesterday, today, and forever. "Jesus Christ is the same yesterday and today and forever" (Hebrews 13:8 NIV).

When you can give God the pain of the past and stand in the now, you're giving Him full permission to use His power to touch all your hurting places. He knows the woman you could have been and the woman you should be, so He sets about healing and restoring you as you call out to Him. He'll reveal to you who you really are, a daughter of the Most High. You can recover the losses suffered at the hands of your abusers and get back what's been taken from you. Jesus can rebuild you from the inside out and gift back to you self-esteem, self-respect, integrity, and honor.

Be careful not to let those violations take from you the other people you really care about and don't let it sabotage what has come into your life now as a good relationship. You probably won't even recognize you're setting your own self up to sabotage something good, so keep your eyes open for that one. As far as relationships go, be careful because it's pretty easy to go from bad guy to bad guy.

The temptation to listen to someone who tells you he wants you and that you're exactly who he's been waiting for is huge. But in reality words are cheap. Don't let words that come from someone's mouth, perhaps someone you may not even really know, be stronger than what the Lord reveals to you by the Holy Spirit. The enemy wants nothing more than to change your destiny, but God can restore you to wholeness. Become triumphant in your destiny, and God will forever be your deliverer.

I can almost see you sitting there and wondering how it will all turn out. How will it happen? How will I be better? Well, it took a considerable amount of my life to finally find out how, but I'm praying I can help your situation by revealing not only my story but also my healing. One thing I definitely learned through this massive process was that bringing person after person into your life is not the way to go. God's healing within you is sometimes inhibited by adding others into the situation. It's much like majoring in mathematics in college. A couple of times a day the professor may throw in some fundamental information about science. It's confusing and unclear, and it takes away the availability of seeing the purpose. If you've been through a circumstance that leaves you wounded, you need time to heal and time to gather up your resources without adding something or someone to your life. Get strong first and let God lead you.

Before my healing began, my baggage of personal hurts and sorrow from loss and lost opportunities grew from a handbag to several large trunks. The longer I dragged those trunks around, the more used to them I got. It was my normal way to travel through the day, carrying all my junk with me. Your friends and family members shouldn't be expected to indulge you based on your large travel bags. You don't really want to be that person to them. You don't want your life to only reflect suffering, ugly temperament, and sadness. There's more to you than that. "But he was pierced for our transgressions, he was crushed for our iniquities; the punishment that brought us peace was on him, and by his wounds we are healed" (Isaiah 53:5 NIV).

This Scripture in Isaiah is talking about Christ on the cross, and those words don't say that by His wounds we *were* healed. It says by His wounds we *are* healed. It's always in the present tense. Jesus has already paid that price for you, and that debt will never come due again. When you begin to walk through your days with Jesus, you develop an understanding of love and trust. His help may come disguised as a thought or a revelation, or it may come in a benevolent act based on the obedience of someone else; however, it's all His choosing. That's the time you begin to understand that your past should not dictate the outcome of your future. God will bring wholeness to your life, and with time the frailties and deficiencies of your life will become mended and put right.

God will never leave you to live life alone. Whether you've been abused sexually or emotionally or physically, you know now that you never have to feel again like you're just out there with no one beside you. "God is our refuge and strength, an ever-present help in trouble. Therefore we will not fear, though the earth give way and the mountains fall into the heart of the sea, though it's waters roar and foam and the mountains quake with their surging" (Psalm 46:1–3 NIV).

That Scripture is mighty. It says that even though the earth is giving way and the mountains are falling around you, you should not fear because God is your refuge and strength. Be united with Him. Let Him be that partner for you, that ever-present help during trouble. If He loves you so much He let His Son give His blood and life for you, you can trust Him.

If no one else had been alive on earth but you, Jesus would still have died and given His life for you because His love is so complete and genuine. So don't be afraid. Talk to Him about everything and take shelter under His wings.

This next portion of Chapter 33 comes to you in the form of a letter written by a friend. It concerns an area of abuse that I can't speak about because I have not lived it, but I believe in my heart that it needs to be included. This is her story of abuse, healing, and the testimony of a reconstructed life. It's her prayer that the wounded person who has not yet felt a thorough healing process would be able to find the needed help, healing, and peace.

The Story of Olivia

The more I listen to women, the more I hear the same pain just in a different light. There may be one who's been abused or used or one who's been beaten down or beat up, but the story is the same ... but different. All abusers use the same cycles. The first cycle is a wooing, which involves their attempt at gaining your trust. The second is a honeymoon period, which infers that everything is okay, all is good, and they stir up in you the feeling that you're very special. The last cycle is the actual abuse and all the pain it involves.

It's a sad fact that not all abuse can be seen with the eye, but all abuse leaves scars. Some of those scars are so deep and ugly they deform the personality. Although no one sees it outwardly on the body, it causes the abused to see only through the veil of ugliness. Some of the scars are covered up with makeup but not the kind you wear on your face. It's a makeup made out of a fake life. Many times on that made up fake life, they wear a fake smile and maybe even have a way of carrying themselves so no one guesses their pain.

We all have choices to make in life; however, very seldom do your choices just affect you. They'll also affect the other people in your life in the future as well as in your present.

Try tossing a rock into a pond and watch the ripples as they multiply and get bigger the farther out they go. Well, an abused life is somewhat the same. The pain and the effects of the abuse ripple and continue to make ripples until her entire life is viewed within the pattern. One example of that revolves around the divorce of my mom and dad when I was a very young child. Had that not happened, I'd have grown up knowing my natural dad and his family. Would I have been abused? Only God knows the answer to that question, but I like to think the answer would be no.

Another example was when my mom married her second husband, a man she knew but one her family warned her about. As a result of her choice to go ahead and marry him, all of her children's lives were damaged in the process, not to mention her own. So not only did the rock get tossed into the pond, but all of our lives and all of our futures were changed forever too.

The Rock

My young life was filled with a variety of people, and one of these people was my funny and very goofy babysitter. She was close to my family, and I was around three years old on this particular day when she was watching me. After I asked her permission, I took her black Labrador dog out for a walk by myself, and instead of me walking it, the dog walked me. Needless to say, I came back to her with tears and bloody knees.

On another day this same lady was babysitting again. She had to go outside, and she left instructions that specifically said I was not to get on the step stool that was next to the heater. Now mind you, I was a three-year-old with a great imagination. I had been playing secretary that day and pretending I was answering the phone. Well, as you guessed it, I was messing around and fell on the hot heater and badly burned myself.

As it happened, this was the very same person who was in charge of watching me when a car rolled over my leg. I'd been playing with a neighbor boy out in the yard, and he decided to get in our car. When he did, he let the emergency brake off. The car rolled back just enough to catch my leg. In remembering these occasions, I realized I'd learned the hard way. I'd learned that life is tough and those tough places and happenings are brought on by choices. It's all really a matter of choices, whether they're yours or someone else's.

Wooing and Honeymoon

After the marriage of my mom, we moved across the United States to be with my new stepfather, Mario, who was in the service. After a very long journey we finally met up with him and settled into our rented house and into our new lives. It was good for the first year, and I loved it because we only lived about a block from the ocean. Mario loved to fish, and I just loved the water and the waves. The beaches aren't like California because you could walk out for what seemed like forever when the tide was out. Mario would grin and pick me up and put me up on his shoulders and then walk out as far as I wanted.

Abuse

One day my stepdad got a job that allowed for him to be home during the day, and that's when everything changed. He was very strict in his rules, and the more he was at home, the more we kids began to see the real person Mom had married. He took delight in scaring us and not always in a fun way, but that was really when the mind games started. Or you could say that's when the mental abuse and the manipulation began.

My mom was not the type of person who yelled, so that definitely wasn't the standard behavior in our house. Mario had a loud and deep voice, so when he yelled, you felt it go right through you. An immediate fear would grip you, and you could never tell what was going to happen next. If he saw that you were afraid, he'd laugh it off and act like everything was just a joke and then say, "I wouldn't hurt you. You can trust me."

I was never spanked by him or my mom, but I can't say that for my other siblings. I was younger. To be truthful, they both had smart mouths, and it got them into trouble. But still their punishment was something that was difficult to witness as a child.

It wasn't until we moved back to California that the real nightmare began for me. People are always talking about normal, but you know, what is normal anyway? I'm not really sure there is such a thing. When you grow up being molested, you don't know what normal is. You hope that maybe your situation is common, but you still know inside that what's happening isn't really what should happen.

It's not until you reach a certain age that you become aware of the difference between an adult's right and wrong and a child's right and wrong. As children, it's the adults who tell us what's right and what's wrong, and since we don't know the difference, we believe them. As we grow, we begin to question that because we hear the adults tell us something that's wrong, and then we see them doing that very thing. It totally gives mixed messages to a child, especially when that child is trying to normalize her life.

The molester makes you feel special in every way at first, and this is part of that wooing cycle, the special gifts and favors. I was too young to realize the price I'd have to pay for this special treatment.

You also don't understand that every time the abuser says he loves you, he isn't saying it with a fatherly love. He's saying it with a perverted lust. You believe what he says to you. After all, he must love you more than the others because he's repeatedly told you how special you are. He goes after your trust by giving you things, important things. He may tell you about a surprise for your mom that you can't tell her about, and that in itself makes you feel special. He watches you obey him, and he knows you'll do what he says, so now he has you right where he needs you. That's where the wooing has ended and the honeymoon has already begun.

The day comes when the abuser touches you and waits for your reaction. He may ask you, "Don't you trust me?" Well, my goodness, he's an adult, and he's asking a child if she trusts him. Something is definitely wrong, but a child is just too innocent and naive to understand it. But it's then he'll look and act hurt if you say anything other than yes, you trust him. Now you have to remember the manipulation of trust that's led up to this point in time. You've been made to feel special, and then you're manipulated into trusting this person. Now that's another act of being treated special. Inside, that child suffers confusion and is unsure of what to feel or do or even think about what is happening. The reaction all depends on what age the child is when she comes into physical contact with the molester.

If as a baby you are hit in the arm every day, you will think that's normal until you're old enough to be around other kids and see that they don't get hit like you do. When you see that others aren't getting hit, you may feel like something's wrong with you, not the adult who's been hitting you all your life. You grow up thinking those other kids are normal, but you're not.

For me I was six or so when the touching started. It wasn't often, but it was enough that I began to wonder if it had been an accident or done on purpose. I remembered watching him to see if he touched anyone else, but he was always so sly and quick about it that it just made me feel odd.

Even at the age of six, my mom insisted I take naps, and they happened at the same time as my stepdad napped. I'd have to lie right there on the bed next to him. Even if I wasn't tired, my mom would tell me to lie there until he went to sleep before I got up. Remember those ripples? They come from choices either made by you or made for you.

I was approximately eight when my stepdad began wanting to check me to see how much I had begun to develop. It just got worse from there. About the age of thirteen it changed significantly. He had been satisfied up to that point just touching me, but he tired of that and wanted me to do the same to him. About a year after that the rapes started.

One of my strategies was to leave my mind and go somewhere safe. When he started forcing himself on me, I learned to listen and be watchful of the times when my mom even looked like she was going out of the house. I'd do this even if she was just going down the street to visit. I learned to disappear if I could and only show up again when I saw my mom come back.

Everything a molester or abuser does is done in stages. Each new stage brings more, and with that, worse threats and verbal abuse. Of course, you feel less special and less loved, and you begin to feel more like an object to take care of his sick lust.

He began to make threats. He said telling on him would do no good because no one would ever believe me over him. He even said that if I told my mom and my siblings, we would all end up in the poorhouse, and it would be my fault. We didn't have much, and we lived on the poor side of town. But my mom was proud. That would have put her over the top. He knew that, and so did I.

The molester and abuser tears down any and all self-worth you may have ever had. The declaration from him that I couldn't do anything as good as anyone else became a normal thing to hear. He would make me watch sporting events with him, and whenever females were involved, he would tear me down and proceed to tell me I could never be that good. It was always the same. No matter the sport, he would tell me that I'd never be as good. I remember asking my mom why I had to watch them with him, and she said it was because she didn't want to hear him complain to her. It wasn't until I was able to get out from under his control that I became determined to set out to prove him wrong in any way I could find. If he had said I couldn't, I was determined to show him I could.

Deliverance

My deliverance from this nightmare came about after my mom and stepdad decided to move out of state. They had taken a trip to visit some friends, and while they were there, they were talked into moving. My mom got really excited and began talking to us about the high school we were going to attend. Later she admitted she was worried about me because I was a girl. At this very high school one of the girls had been beaten up so badly that her face was unrecognizable to her own mother. I asked my mom if she had lost her mind and then told her if she moved me there, I would refuse to go to school. That was a harsh moment for me and really sad because I had been trying really hard to finish school early so that I could move out of their house. Where we lived then had been the longest we had ever lived anywhere. I had made friends. I knew who the bad kids were, and I knew who the safe ones were.

Our school was so bad that they had security guards on campus to keep the gangs separated, and now my mom wanted me to move to yet another type of nightmare. For the first time in my life I rebelled. I didn't want to live with my stepdad, and I didn't want to go to that nightmare of a school. But after what I had lived through, what else could they do to me?

The family I babysat for graciously said I could stay with them, but my mom wouldn't allow that. She was worried about what people would think of her as a mother. We talked until we came up with a compromise. It was finally settled. I was going to go stay with a relative who only lived a couple of hours away. But that was short-lived because several months later my mom told me I had to come home. She said she needed help with the younger one. So after all my feelings of rebellion and then assuming the settlement of compromise, it all came down to the fact that I would still have to move back in the house with him. However, this time my stepdad never touched me again. I lived there approximately six months before I left my mom's house to go live with my natural dad and his mom, and that is where I met the man I eventually married.

Summation of My View of Life While Growing Up

After my mom married my stepdad, our family moved more than thirteen times within approximately twelve years. I was that new kid in class in each of the new schools I attended. Because of the moves, we didn't live long enough in any location for me to make good connections with friends. I missed out on having sleepovers, going to church camp, and most of all, the regular activities that occur in a child's life.

We were poor most of the time I lived at home. Being poor meant I always had to wear hand-me-down clothes from relatives and my older sister. I remember having shoes that were so worn that they had cardboard on the inside to cover the holes in the bottom. I felt like I was a throwaway child.

Growing up in an abusive home and not being able to really connect with anyone gave me a feeling that there was no one I could trust. The abusive manner in the home, the molestations, and the rapes all left me with literally no feelings of worth, no self-esteem, and thoughts of shattered dreams. Feelings of hopelessness and loneliness were with me throughout my earlier life. I began blaming myself for everything that went wrong, and thoughts of suicide and murder of my abuser ran through my head.

God's Healing

You may be wondering how I ever overcame my past. There were times in my life when I didn't think that was possible, but I can happily say that today I am a healed and whole person. That abused and mixed-up little girl who lived in my heart was evicted. Now I am a daughter of the Most High because of the love of my God, who kept me safe.

I began going through counseling, and I would hear horrible stories from other women. I can only say, "Thank You, Lord," because I found out my life could have been so much worse than it was. It took years of prayer and learning to forgive.

God has continued to heal me because I chose to let Him. I knew that for my healing to happen, I needed to trust God and believe in Him and rely solely on Him.

I used to think I was a survivor. But actually the word *survivor* means remaining alive after a dangerous event. Now I know that what I really am is a conqueror. That is someone who takes control to defeat someone or something. Through the years God has shown me how to gain control over my life, and now I choose how I want to live. I'm now a wife and mother of two grown boys, and I have five beautiful grandchildren. And yes, while I was growing up, I asked the Lord why it had to happen, but He never revealed that. Because God began to teach me how to trust Him without question, it has all turned out all right.

I prayed and asked the Lord to remove all the ugly and harmful damage that the devil had meant for my life, and then I asked God to turn it into good for me and for those whose lives I would be able to touch. It was my prayer that God would let me see my stepdad with the same eyes as He saw him.

I knew that my mom had been weak, and there were periods of time during my counseling when I just sort of had to walk away from her. But she became ill, and when no one came forward to help her, I made the choice to be there for her. I believe God honored my prayer to take the bad and use it for good, and as a result of taking care of her, it seemed to make me stronger.

As a consequence of my new strength, I was able to forgive my stepdad for the evil he had done to me. I tried to show him Christ in my life. Approximately two years before he passed, I prayed with him, and he did come to know the Lord. I made those choices to forgive because I wanted to be forever free from the pain, and God walked with me all the way through the entire process.

I have found that God still continues to help and heal me when I use my experiences to help others. In fact, while I was putting together this story, God continued to reveal memories of things I'd simply forgotten. Sometimes now when others look at me, it's hard for them to believe I'm that same person I talk about in my story. All the healing in my life is because of my heavenly Father's love, and I give God all the glory.

I'm grateful to my friend for including my life in this book because it allowed me to walk through the journey with her. Together we found that it doesn't matter what name is on the abuse. It all has the same ending, a broken and wounded person. Together my friend and I have taken our brokenness to the cross and received our healings, and through the power of Jesus Christ, we are more than conquerors. I pray that through the healing power of Jesus Christ, you are also able to receive your healing. *To God be all the glory!*

Chapter
34

No Condemnation

Throughout this book I've tried to honestly guide you through who the Lord has become to me and the mighty things He's brought into my life. Condemnation or actually a lack of condemnation has played a big part in that.

To condemn means to place blame, guilt, or rebuke, to find fault or criticize. But God says in Romans 8:1, there is *now* no condemnation for those who are in Christ Jesus. The way that verse is written, no matter when you read it, it's talking about the present. That means when you read it the first time and when you read it the last time, it will be current for that moment.

There are lots of people who talk about the condemnation of God and believe He's constantly mad and disappointed, thinking of mankind as a failing people. They hold Old Testament beliefs tight to their heart. But that doesn't allow for the grace and mercy that comes with the sacrifice of Jesus as shown in the New Testament. God does not think about you that way, and He doesn't treat you that way. His plan for you is solid and good, and He only wants the best for you, His child.

God's choices are productive and always bring about a beneficial solution; however, they may not match how you would have accomplished this task. He has compassion for you, and according to Isaiah 30:18, God also longs to be gracious to you.

The initial sin of disobedience, which Adam and Eve committed, caused a separation between God and His people. Basically the only way I can attempt to explain this is to simply say that Jesus has always been and always will be God. He is one-third of the Holy Trinity. In heaven He offered to be birthed into an earthly form as a baby. Over two thousand years ago, that's exactly what happened. Jesus was born of a human mother who was a virgin, but He was fathered by the Holy Spirit. Joseph was only His earthly dad. Because He is God, that made Him our Redeemer and Savior, and because He was on earth, He was able to carry out that function. That is why He is referred to as the Son of God.

Now according to Leviticus 17:11, the life of the creature is in the blood, and it's the giving of the blood on the altar that makes atonement for one's life. That's exactly what Christ was doing for you, making atonement. In Romans 3:25, it says God presented Christ as a sacrifice of atonement through faith in His blood.

In death on the cross, He took with Him all the sins, diseases, sicknesses, infirmities, grief, pain, sorrows, and much more. He took it all, and through that blood sacrifice, He restored the relationship between man and God. You are now free to walk and talk with the Lord just as Adam and Eve did twenty-four hours a day about anything and everything.

Jesus became your redemption, your salvation, your deliverance, and your rescue. Because He is God, His blood was worthy of being that sacrifice for you. His sacrifice on the cross allows you eternal access to your Father. It also allows you freedom from the bondage and penalty of sin and sickness. Now when God looks at you, He doesn't see you in your sin. He sees you through Jesus' righteous blood. He sees you through that perfect blood sacrifice that never has to be given again. The price is paid. The guilt is gone. However, if you choose to sin, you will find consequences staring you in the face.

After you ask forgiveness and repent of your sin, if you continue to feel ashamed and punish yourself for those same sins that will allow the enemy to work against you. In actuality you've just handed him ammunition to use against yourself, based on your own thoughts and words.

If you've truly repented, don't allow yourself to think and feel you're not righteous in God's sight. Don't let His sacrifice become meaningless. The enemy can't read your mind, but he can certainly hear your voice and watch how you act. Listening to what you moan and groan about and what you tell your friends gives him all the ammunition he needs. He'll lay every guilt trip on you that he can. The enemy will take the fact that Jesus took on the ultimate price for your sins on the cross and then turn that around. He will do everything in his power to place guilt on you because you haven't stopped sinning. Then he'll try to dump a big load of shame in your lap while he's telling you that you're weak and you've failed God. Don't let him do that to you.

Because of the sin of Adam and Eve, everyone birthed after them was born into a sinful world. It certainly doesn't mean you have to sin, but it means that the influence of sin lives all around you, and because of that sphere of sinful influence, you are certainly vulnerable to it. One of the things I believe that's very typical of this influence is the pressure and persuasion coming from friends.

For example, your friends may think that sex outside of marriage is perfectly fine or that having an abortion might be your answer for your unplanned pregnancy. They may have even encouraged you to get a divorce because you think you've fallen out of love. Listening to the worldly influence encourages you to make different life choices than prayer might have. Sin-based, short-term decisions bring all kinds of possible long-term consequences.

I just mentioned abortion as an alternative that your friends might give to you as a way out of an unplanned pregnancy. My personal belief is that the Scriptures are very clear about that, saying that taking of an innocent life is a sinful act. I myself am not willing to risk the possible long-term consequences of that action, and I pray you won't either. If you did make that choice, my heart breaks for you, and I want you to know that God is very clear in His forgiveness. He offers that forgiveness to you as His child. As a believer, all you have to do to receive is be truly repentant. Talk to God about it and tell Him how you feel. You don't have to make excuses. Just talk to Him and then release it from your mind and your heart's emotion. Do not let the enemy taunt you, ever again. If guilt comes back into your thoughts regarding this situation after you've repented, just know that this comes straight from the lying tongue of the enemy.

Many people have made horrible decisions or decisions they thought were right and found out later weren't, including me. Then there's always those who weren't believers when they made those incorrect decisions and now wish they could take them back. Yep, it's too bad there's not an erase button, but God's got it all. He has a plan for everything because He knows you. He knows the real you. He knew you before you were born, and He still has that plan for you.

God forgives every sin that you offer up in repentance, and it doesn't matter what it is. Absolutely nothing is too big for God, and don't let anyone take that from you, including yourself. God will take what the enemy means for evil and turn it around and use it for His good. His purpose is for you to be restored.

The Lord also doesn't want to be left out of your choices. He's right there with you all the time. You just may not see Him. He's waiting for you to ask Him to help, but don't forget to wait for His answer, no matter how long it takes. There'll be times when it seems like forever to you, but He may be moving things around and working things out for you in heavenly places. Trust that He has your best interest at heart and don't make short-term decisions. Wait until you've prayed and have total peace.

If you've been asked to make a choice and it's a life choice, especially one involving a man, and you think you don't have time to pray and wait, I would say step back and don't go there. If the end result is something God wants for you, He can still work it out if you pray and wait in expectation. I speak from experience when I tell you that God chooses His own timing, and I also know that His timing isn't anything like what you'd expect. Try not to even guess because that might just be the one thing that causes you to begin to doubt. It's not because He wants to punish you or show you who is boss. It's because He knows everything and everyone involved. When you ask Him to give you His choice, He'll want you to wait for His perfect answer. He sets things in motion so that it all ends up right and good, but the timing issue isn't yours. It's His. Sometimes it may be that it's okay with God, and He'll answer immediately. Other times He may make you wait. He wants to know if you really understand what you're asking and if you're sincere and in His will. But whatever the cost in time, isn't it worth it if you end up with the very best that's been handpicked by God?

In my youth I was never one of those children who had an imaginary best friend no one else could see. Because of that, it's probably harder for me to understand how those little ones experienced their relationship with those special, unseen friends. But as I'm sharing this with you, I imagine that their feeling is probably somewhat like the feeling I get about God. God is with me all the time, and even though no one sees Him, that doesn't mean He's not there. He is there, and He's my best friend.

Your husband or your child can't be your *best* friend. I know that sounds harsh, and you may immediately feel that I'm wrong. But you have to put God first. It has to be Him. He has to be in first place in your life. When you actually put God in His place, you'll quickly understand that nothing gets taken from your other relationships. In fact, your love for your spouse and your children becomes deeper. You'll find you have more to give because you have God as your example of a true loving and meaningful connection and bond.

It's the enemy who tries to trick you into believing that you've separated yourself from God when you sin and that you're unworthy. If you listen to his lies, he'll have you believing you can't achieve victory over your behavior or your attitude or your habits. He wants you to think that God is mad at you and things will never change, but that is so totally untrue. When a negative thought comes into your mind and it doesn't line up with what God says, discard it immediately and go on. You haven't sinned by having that sinful thought come to you, but if you take it and run with it, then you've made a choice to sin. The fix is to be repentant and remorseful in your confession, letting God know you understand you've done wrong and you want to change so that you don't repeat it.

Jesus Christ is the one who already died to pay for your sins, so as a believer, you won't be judged or condemned for them. There's no guilt and no penalty. His sacrifice paid that penalty and took on that condemnation, and that's what allows you to stand in righteousness before God's presence. Your obedience didn't have anything to do with making you righteous, and your disobedience won't cause you to lose righteousness. Your righteousness only comes through the blood of Jesus Christ. God wants your attempts at the best you have, and He blesses and gives favor to those who walk with Him.

I've found that when you're going through difficult times and trying to get a type of relief or rescue, you can't afford to be guided by ugly moods and attitudes. Don't pay attention to others who might question what may be happening in your life if you're waiting on an answer from God. Don't let them sway your thinking. Let God determine your course. Be confident, and as long as you know it's God who is leading you, just go with it. Attitudes of doubt and defensiveness make you vulnerable, so just disregard them.

So when negative, evil, or hurtful thoughts come to your mind, recognize what spirit they've come from. In the world there's only God's side and the enemy's side, just two spiritual factions that rule and reign. Everything, even if it seems of no consequence, comes from or stems from one of those factions. There's no neutral ground, and you don't have to keep thoughts just because they're presented to you. You have all authority, through Jesus to tell the enemy to get lost. But that only works in real life if you in truth believe in the authority given to you, through Christ. Speak God's Word with authority, pray with authority, read your Bible with authority, and tell others what God's teaching you with that same authority.

I spent many years thinking I was incapable of sharing and incapable of having real authority in Christ. I'd lived so many years of wrong choices and made so many mistakes that I just did not trust my own knowledge about anything. Now I've come to realize that most of those concepts about myself reared their ugly heads because of my horrible self-image. I let the enemy have a field day with me, and I'd allowed him to beat me down. He took years from my life because I let him. He repeatedly told me that I was to blame, that I should be ashamed. Wasn't it embarrassing that everyone who knew me knew how stupid I'd been?

Please don't do that to yourself. Let Jesus be your best friend. He died for you. He gave everything for you just because of His total love for you. Don't let that be inconsequential in your life. By the way, if the Lord loves you and says you're righteous and wants to give you Himself, isn't that all that really matters?

Having Christ's authority allows you to tell that ugly devil to go away, get out, and stop bothering you. You don't always need to go to the point of rebuking the enemy, although I'm not telling you not to do this. What I am saying is that if he's bugging you, use the authority Christ gave you and just tell him to get lost, but don't forget to do it in the name of Jesus. If you know you need backup, by all means call out to Jesus and ask Him for help. If needed, call out for the Lord to send every angel necessary to come to your aid.

Matthew 4:2–11 talks about when Jesus fasted for forty days and the devil tried to tempt Him. Jesus really didn't even give the enemy the time of day. His basic response was, "It is written," and then He offered up to the devil the Word of God. He stayed firm, and He didn't give excuses or take the time to prove His point. He just said it with true knowledge and His authority. Christ has given you that same authority, but if you don't exercise it and gain strength in its purpose, it won't mean anything. It will just be words. Believe me when I say that the enemy doesn't respond to just words. He responds to the authority behind the words. So find out what you really know, build your strength of faith, become strong in the Lord, and put the enemy under your feet.

Anytime self-pity, offense, worry, guilt, shame, and suffering try to wheedle their way into your thoughts, recognize those as coming from the bad spiritual faction. The good side, God's side, wants to bring peace, love, joy, strength, determination, and acceptance. Yes, you may be bent a little from your struggles, but with the Lord's healing touch, you'll get straight again. So don't look back. Look forward and begin to renew your mind and take control. Don't ever let the enemy or even your past begin to determine your future because the Lord already has your future waiting for you.

Chapter
35

Am I His Favorite?

In Genesis 1:1, it says in the beginning God created the heavens and the earth, but it doesn't say *in God's beginning*. Humans don't generally have an understanding of how it can be that God didn't begin somewhere. But that doesn't make it any less true. If God says He's always existed, even though I don't understand it, I believe it. "The secret things belong to the LORD our God, but the things revealed belong to us and to our children forever, that we may follow all the words of this law" (Deuteronomy 29:29 NIV).

The most wonderful gift God has given to you is Himself. He has all the time in the world for you and desperately adores and treasures you. There's nothing about you He doesn't know or care about. He longs to be with you and yearns for that enthusiastic companionship with His created one. It doesn't bother Him when you come with your questions because you're hungry for knowledge. He's committed to you, and He wants you to come before Him even in your times of emotional turmoil and when you're full of tears. He doesn't think you're boring, He sees you as valuable and beautiful. He loves you so much that He collects your tears in a bottle and He sings over you, delighting Himself in you.

"You keep track of all my sorrows. You have collected all my tears in your bottle. You have recorded each one in your book" (Psalm 56:8 NLT). "The LORD your God is with you, the Mighty Warrior who saves. He will take great delight in you; in his love he will no longer rebuke you, but will rejoice over you with singing" (Zephaniah 3:17 NIV). These Scriptures exhibit the perfect knowledge God has of you along with the intense care He takes with all of His creations, particularly you. He delights in you, and His love for you is deep and strong. Not a single hair would fall to the ground without His knowledge. That's how well He watches over you. "And even the very hairs of your head are all numbered. So don't be afraid; you are worth more than many sparrows" (Matthew 10:30–31 NIV).

My friend and I have a fun thing we do every now and then. I'll look over at her and say, "You know I'm God's favorite," and then she says, "No, I'm His favorite. He said so." I just look right back at her, and with a big grin I say, "No, He just told you that because He didn't want to hurt your feelings. I'm really the favorite." And then we just laugh and laugh.

We laugh because we know that somehow we're both His favorite. All His children are His favorites. That's the wonderful thing about our Lord. He has the capacity to operate as if He is in an intimate and loving relationship with you and yet fulfill that same lovely connection with each and every one of His children. He accomplishes this all at the same time. I don't know about you, but I'm in awe of my God. I love being His favorite.

> Your eyes saw my unformed body; all the days ordained for me were written in your book before one of them came to be.
>
> —Psalm 139:16 NIV

Chapter
36

Sons and Daughters

Everything in this manual has been collected through different life phases, and this writing is the culmination of that life to this point. I've been waiting to get to this chapter because I need to thank my children for the love and support they've shown to me throughout their lives. I want to let them know they've been my anchor, that steadfast part of my life, the part that was meaningful and couldn't be taken away.

I didn't know when I was raising my kids how to let God be my defender, protector, guide, Father, daddy, partner, husband, or friend, but He had always been my God and my Savior. I had no inkling as to how to let Him rule and reign in my life and how to accept His love for me. But my love for Him was no less real, and I tried to show that to them.

While I was growing up, I wished to have two children, first a boy and then a girl. I'd always wanted an older brother in my life, so I really hoped I'd have a son first. I wanted my daughter to have someone in front of her to act as a protector and guide in life. Fortunately both of my children, who were fathered by Husband #1, came in that order. First there was my handsome son, and eighteen months later my beautiful daughter arrived.

In this portion of my story it's essential to explain something to both my children and to you, the reader, in the hopes that you won't make the same dreadful mistake I've made. I want to start off by saying that I definitely did not go about making life choices in the correct way. I didn't pray about most of them, and I either wasn't asking God for help or wasn't waiting long enough for His answers.

It's a hard concept to convey, especially to your own children, that you didn't plan for them. Nor were the pregnancies timed well. Like others, I have made huge mistakes, and one of them was the way I handled my conversations regarding this specific issue. I've said so many times in my life that I've made wrong choices in my marriages and that these choices changed my life forever. I'd heard myself say I wasn't ready for a baby and was caught totally unaware when I found myself pregnant with my son. I just tried not to think about it. I'd mentioned the timing was all wrong when I got pregnant with my daughter and how that impacted my life. I had shared those comments many times.

Not too long ago I was sitting in the car with my granddaughter. My daughter, her mother, was in the car with us. Because my granddaughter was beginning her adult life, I was encouraging her to make wise choices. I went into great explanation of the depth of pain and hurt that can happen if there are wrong choices made in youthful decisions. I explained that once those decisions were made, it was too late for other options, and life would just carry on. We talked for a while, and then the discussion moved into options regarding husbands. Without thinking, I went right into my preaching of my results of my bad choices. My daughter waited for a minute and then stopped me and said, "Well, Mom, if you had made different choices,

I wouldn't be here. I wouldn't be alive." When I heard that come out of her mouth, I winced. It almost ripped my heart out when I thought how easily that just flew off my tongue without regard for who was involved in the entire story.

That revelation of what I had apparently expressed to both of my children hit me like a big boulder. I had never thought of them as taking my words and keeping in their heart the feeling that they were accidents and therefore unwanted. I'd never considered how redoing my marriage choices may have impacted these particular children of mine. In fact, they may not have been born to me, and they may have belonged to someone else.

Oh, my goodness, how many years had my children heard this confession from me? I never one time put them in as players in my story and never thought about how they would perceive my statements. I had never taken those situations and thought about how I would feel if the story was turned around and that was said about me. But whether I planned it or not, my kids lived for years thinking those very things. I would never have given to them those feelings on purpose; however, I had done so by accident.

I would like to say to my children, that I'm sorry I hurt your heart all those years. I'm sorry that you felt the sting of my regrets in life, and I'm sorry I wasn't more wise in how I expressed myself to you and to others. As far as choices are concerned, I made them, good and bad, and I would gladly go back and do it all over again just to have you as my children in my life.

You see, my children and grandchildren are my loves. I would never let them go. They are mine, and I pray for their lives and for their safety and protection always.

In some of the words and phrasing I chose to use during the previous chapters in regard to my early life, you'll find me using terminology that suggests what we've just been talking about. I've chosen to keep that part of my story the same because it explains the old me perfectly. That was how I lived, and those were my thoughts. Throughout this story it's been important for you to understand what I was faced with and how I felt about that. I wanted you to know why I was personally drawn into walking through my life with blame, shame, guilt, and regret.

Of course, I'm not really at liberty to talk in depth about the majority of it. I do, however, believe in my heart that what I've revealed to you will provide you with a perception of my story and what was needed to be heard. What's truly remarkable is that even as I come toward the end of my story in a chapter about my children, the Lord is still revealing to me the healing happening in my life.

Sometimes I'm amazed at how one woman could have become so messed up, but praise God that I'm redeemed and liberated. I feel as if I have new breath in my life. My prayer is that He continues to put before me women to share my story with in the hopes of their healing. In addition to that, I pray the Lord will guide me and prepare me to do my sharing without exposing my children to unwise or careless speech.

I pray if any of you out there reading this have carelessly hurt your loved ones with your words or even your actions, I hope that you will take the time to stop and ask for forgiveness from them and from your heavenly Father. That's a really big step into a new life and a new way of expression, and that choice will only bring continued healing to you and restoration and peace to them.

Chapter
37

Repentance

In looking back at my life, I realize there were many times when I should have treated situations much differently. Left to itself, sin always has the capacity to change your life. Had I been closer with the Lord, the Holy Spirit could have enlightened me about the direction I was headed in when I automatically assumed guilt. This automatic assumption should have been a definite red light because it never allowed clarification about who was responsible or even what portion of responsibility should have been mine.

There are marriage partners who have behavior traits that not only permit but almost demand that you accept blame for every situation. Of course, that makes the load that you carry way too heavy. Sometimes you become overwhelmed with just trying to lug it around, and frustration will become your new friend. But the Lord never intended for you or anyone to carry guilt around. Because repentance is all about the desire to avoid repeating that action, how could it be possible for you to be truly repentant for something you didn't take part in?

It's good for your soul and advantageous to your mental health when you're able to really pick apart what happened and decide if you were even partially responsible. If you were, then take care of it. Then ask the Lord to give you guidance and strength to stop this pattern of automatically accepting everyone's blame as if it were your own. Listen to your words and try to catch how many times you say, "I'm sorry." It's something inside of you that's causing this thinking that you've failed in some area and that you must be partially or wholly responsible. God can help you get it sorted out and changed and healed. Letting go of all that pent up emotion and culpability is very freeing. Don't allow anyone to coerce or compel you into carrying liability for simply having imperfections and weaknesses.

My suggestion is to be totally honest with God and break it all down and let Him show you what inside of you may be causing this. Personally I've found that when I'm honest with God and just tell Him that I don't know why and I don't know how but that I need help, He steps in and begins to work and heal. The Lord won't override you. You have to want it, and that starts with surrender and sometimes forgiveness. If there's an issue and it needs to be forgiven, then do it, and if you need to forgive yourself, do that too. I hope no one misunderstands what I'm trying to say. But in the past I found that a big majority of my problems revolved around me not forgiving myself. Some people have said that you don't have to forgive yourself, but I don't agree. I wasn't letting myself off the hook for anything. If I'd made a wrong decision because I was ignorant of the true facts, then I would hold myself responsible and feel liable maybe forever. The enemy never failed to bring those things back to my memory so that I could spend time dwelling on them. Not forgiving and not having a repentant heart will tie God's hands. Actually it ties yours too. When it's time, the Lord will reveal to you the how and the why, and then your pattern of behavior will begin to change. Once that process starts, healing begins.

Having a relationship with the Holy Spirit is vital because it's the Holy Spirit who teaches you how to listen for His warnings and promptings and how to ignore promptings from the enemy. So be humble and teachable and don't resent accountability. Seek comfort in the grace of God. Remember that through grace and mercy you can be free from the condemnation, criticism, self-reproach, and culpability of your sin, even though you in fact did sin. It's your true repentance that the Lord wants because that's what brings freedom. His desire is to change your heart. Second Corinthians 3:18 says you are being transformed into His likeness with ever-increasing glory, which comes from the Lord.

Chapter
38

Passion and Promise

Have you ever felt like you were missing something, something really big in your life? My children and grandchildren have always been close to my heart and vitally important, but for me I still knew something that was supposed to be in my life was missing. I'm sure if someone asked me, I would have said that I was missing the love of a good man. But after I read and studied the story of the woman at the well in John 4, I knew what I thought I was missing wasn't at all what I was actually missing. I don't even remember how many times I had heard that simple story about the conversation between the Samaritan woman at the well and Jesus. However, every time I heard it, my mind always brought up the same thing. I thought He was attempting to guide her into being saved and becoming a believer. Oh, my goodness, I had gotten only part of it. Why did it take me so long before my spiritual ears finally alerted me to what the Lord was telling her and what He also wanted me to hear?

When Jesus spoke to her about drinking the living water, He actually was placing worth upon her and giving her a value that in her culture would never be available to her. She had five previous husbands and was now living with a man and was not married to him. Jesus was offering her His unconditional love and the promise of an eternal future with Him. He was telling her she needed to give up her quest to have that thirst quenched by others. Jesus wanted her to know He could fill all the areas in her life, all the gaps, and all the sorrows and give her unconditional love and security forever. She would never have to feel that type of need in her life again. He was offering her a forever partner with no conditions in His love and someone who could be that for her always.

When I put together a picture of her in my mind, I began to see the spiritual difference between needing and having. Those of you who've felt as if a part of your very person has been missing shouldn't be looking to others for earthly fulfillment. Instead, recognize the Lord is the one who's always been there and always will be waiting for you, the only one who will quench that thirst.

When I finally pieced this whole scenario together, I realized all along that the Lord had been there for me and desired me to be there for Him. What I had been missing was that adoring, intimate, personal, one-on-one relationship with my heavenly Father. I was missing letting God be to me what I needed Him to be. I was missing letting Him take care of me while allowing myself to rest completely in Him. I was also missing that safe relationship with no fear, no intimidation, no guilt, and no questions, one that you can only have with someone who loves you, without condition.

Now I'm not sure most people can relate to the fears that I talked about earlier. My fear of the dark removed completely any real feeling of security and safeness. But when I gave my fear of the dark and then my fear of the unknown up to my Lord and He accepted those from me, it changed my life forever. The enemy was no longer able to torment me by making me wonder what might happen to me or to my loved ones. He could no longer make me terrified of what I might find in my own house or outside in the yard or in the backseats of my car or anything that movies and television invite into your mind. Even though it sounds as if I'm saying it was just a matter of simply giving my fears over to God, much more was involved. Those fears began when I was a little child, and through the years they accumulated, each year adding to their strength.

As a little girl, singing was the first part of me I recognized as my way to communicate. It was an internal joy in my life, and even though I found myself unable to let go in front of others, inside my head I could. Inside my heart and mind I could be the person I wanted to be. Fairly often I was invited to sing at other churches and local events, and as an adult, I became involved in a local quartet. In fact, I was fortunate enough to sing in vocal groups with both of my sisters at different times. It was special, and I loved it. One year the vocal group my older sister and I sang in was asked to compete in a Christian music competition at the California State Fair. We placed second in the music division for Christian groups. That was a great experience, and I still hold our trophy.

But because of my shyness and total lack of confidence, I had let myself become unprotected. I told no one about my issues and my fear and I certainly never asked for help from anyone. I found myself going through, a not pleasant, physical experience each and every time I tried to perform. I'd allowed the enemy to bring to me a fear that totally consumed any ease I could gather together. I'd become convinced that I'd forget my words on stage, and to someone with no confidence, that was a horrific thought. Putting yourself in a place of total exposure in front of possibly hundreds of people is just the worst when you're fearful. I knew it would be easier to give up than remain in that battle. I finally did give in rather than continue to fight the fear and dread and emotional roller coaster.

I remember I was in my late twenties, when I reached the point of actually giving up singing. I don't mean I gave it up for others. I totally gave it up. I backed out of being involved in any groups, and I no longer accepted invitations to sing all because of fear.

I didn't know it then, but it was the enemy that had been whispering that lie of forgetfulness into my ears. I had just assumed it was because I was a weak person. My ignorance of what the enemy was capable of doing had put handcuffs on me. It had me totally bound in fear. Singing for me had been a joyful part of my life, and giving up on that was very sad. But even more regrettable is the fact that the enemy has been in the process of taking that same joy and pleasure from thousands of other people, and they don't even know it. They don't understand that it doesn't have to be that way. I didn't understand then either. I prayed and prayed and spoke faithfully and then prayed again and rehearsed and prayed some more, but I never could overcome that fear.

I just felt lost. I couldn't find my direction, and I felt as if I had no compass. It wasn't until much later in my life that I became aware that my fear of being left on stage and hoping to find the forgotten words was being sourced through the enemy. I would try to work myself up into speaking positive faith as much as I could, but it never worked. Somewhere in my mind I was still fearful that it wouldn't work, so it didn't. That, my friend, is called doubt, and doubt absolutely stunts any progress.

One day about a year before I met my new Christian friends, I was sitting in church and listening to my interim pastor in my new hometown. He was speaking about the spiritual world and was explaining that God hadn't given us a spirit of timidity but instead had given a spirit of power, of love, and of self-discipline. Now I'd heard of the teaching before, but that morning when he said the words *spirit of timidity*, my heart immediately connected with that. I instantly understood that the spirit of timidity was the enemy that had always been there around me, trying to instill fear in order to control me.

I know now that my realization came straight from the Holy Spirit. The spiritual battle that constantly goes on around you is something you don't see, but when you're connected to the Holy Spirit, somehow you just know.

The evil spirits are fallen (bad) angels that inhabited heaven until they joined the devil in his arrogant and willful disobedience of God. They aren't dead people. So it doesn't have to be a scary, creepy thing, but it is a thing that has to be dealt with in a spiritual way.

When the Holy Spirit revealed to me what my interim pastor was saying, I couldn't wait to get home and take care of some business. I stood in my living room and said out loud, "I know who you are now, so get out, leave me alone, and don't ever come back. In the name of Jesus." I meant every word I said. My faith was huge, and my speech was full of authority. I knew who I was talking to now. I knew it wasn't me that had been the problem, and I was mad. I was really mad. Getting that revelation from the Holy Spirit, that thing you can hang on to and hold and use, is the real thing. It actually made me feel big in the Lord, like that was a solid piece of evidence that was so strong. No one would ever be able to take that away from me. That was how it was that day. It was just over, and it wasn't tough. Once the Holy Spirit revealed to me that it wasn't me, that it wasn't a lack in me, that it wasn't because I wasn't good enough or because I was weak, the fight was over. That blame I'd attached to myself, that blame of not being enough, seemed to lift and just fall off, and I began to sense a permission to hope.

I prayed over my nervousness about forgetting the words to songs. I asked the Lord to gift to me a memory that would not fail me, and I would be able to remember the words to all the songs I'd practiced. I knew with that in my grasp there would be no fear. If I did feel a fearful moment coming, I'd say something like, "Oh no, I'm not going there. Get out," and if I couldn't talk, in the song somewhere I'd add, "Thank You, Jesus." Then it would leave because that spirit knew to whom my faith was speaking and it had to obey the authority behind it. You may be thinking, *That sounds weird*. But it's not weird, and it's not going overboard. It's being real.

The Holy Spirit had revealed to me what I'd been dealing with, and my part of the battle was to wear my armor. I had to protect myself with the shield of faith and wield the sword of the Spirit. All I had to do was speak in faith, and because I had that knowing, that understanding, I had authority through Jesus.

I found it easy to begin again. I was singing to and for myself, singing for church events, on the worship team, in a trio with my younger sister and my niece, and then in a trio with two male Christian friends. That problem has never returned, and it never will. God gifted to me an ease and a joy I'd not had before when I was singing for Him. "For God hath not given us the spirit of fear; but of power, and of love, and of a sound mind" (2 Timothy 1:7 KJV). I discovered that without fear I was able to sing to and for my Lord and not just perform.

What I hadn't discovered was that I could have gotten rid of all the other fears in my life at that same time. But because of the condition and state of my life, it would still take another three years before I would come to the Lord for help with my fear of the dark. "Then your light will break forth like the dawn, and your healing will quickly appear; then your righteousness will go before you, and the glory of the LORD will be your rear guard. Then you will call, and the LORD will answer; you will cry for help, and he will say: Here am I" (Isaiah 58:8–9 NIV).

I hadn't learned yet that it wasn't about being the toughest and best Christian. It was about learning to let God be what I needed Him to be. So in regard to my fears, yes, I needed a protector and a defender I could trust with all my heart. I needed my rearguard. When you have the Creator of the universe as your protector and defender, nothing is impossible. However, there's a stipulation. You have to allow Him to carry it out, and you have to believe He can and will do it.

It became evident to me that it was time to let God work in other areas of my life. I made a decision to open this really big part of my life to the Lord.

I really needed something drastic done in my life regarding the old feelings of neglect, abandonment, and disregard as a woman. I knew this was probably the basic key to resolution in my life. The Lord had revealed to me the wounds in my past and had healed so much already. He had absolutely taken away my fear of the dark and the unknown, but this one was my biggest all-time challenge. This didn't have anything to do with the unknown. This was glaringly evident in my life.

Even though I had given permission to the Lord to begin to deal with it, I immediately felt as if I wanted to backtrack. My friend's statement about me realizing that I would find myself not needing a man was a scary thought. Even though I said I never wanted a man again and felt as if I didn't deserve one and actually still believed there might not be such a thing as a godly husband for me, inside my heart I still hungered for it.

I didn't have a clue what might be involved, but I now knew that the other things my new friend had said were true. So instead of backtracking, I asked the Lord to help me in giving to Him full availability to do whatever it took to get me right.

I still hadn't had any changes in my personal life and didn't really allow myself to think about it, but I was desperately curious about how this could occur. Truly this was going to be the most important and valuable lesson I would ever learn in this life.

It was my new Christian friend who had helped me recognize the mistakes I had established in my relationships and with those persons I'd allowed into my personal life. He kick-started my desire to change, and now I believed that it could actually happen to me. But just having knowledge and knowing the truth doesn't take you anywhere unless you're willing to start to walk it out. Not just have the knowledge of the faith to do it, but walking in the process of the steps of faith. Because the Lord knew I was serious about this new step and because I knew how much it would drastically change my relationships on earth as well as my relationship with the Lord, I figured this one was probably going to hurt.

I'm not going to say that you should be careful what you ask God to do in your life, but I will say you'd better be ready. What the Lord revealed to me next was about His desire for me to stay passionate with Him. I knew this was going to be vital to whatever the Lord was going to teach me, but I had always believed I had stayed passionate with Him, so now I was confused. When I heard that word from the Lord, it was as if He was telling me He recognized I had a love for Him and a desire to learn about Him, but what He desired from me was much more. Realizing that apparently He wanted more than I had been giving, kind of hurt my heart. If what I had been giving wasn't enough, then I felt I wasn't sure I knew what staying passionate really was. I began to question if I even had that within me. I'm not simply talking about just not having enough for God. I'm saying I began to wonder if I could even feel that way at all.

By the time of my divorce from Husband #4, I had already done my best to block myself off from deep emotional feelings for most everyone except my very immediate family. I hadn't wanted to get hurt again. Nor was I sure I would be able to recover if I did. Inside my head I stayed closed off, and to be totally truthful, I was probably just mad and angry at it all. Being divorced four times and being single once again, as ugly as it was, was just what I accepted. At least I wasn't setting myself up for disappointment anymore. Now when I was faced with what God wanted from me, I was unsure how much I could even open up to find that passion. I began to question if maybe I had gone too far into my tucking-in and hiding mode. My own self-preservation had blocked me. I began to wonder if I had the same capability for love that the normal people had. I was really mixed up, and I started to think that maybe I had gotten confused. Maybe I had begun in my mind to liken God to a man. Now in reality I knew God was God and not a man, but He is always talked about like a man. I began to consider that my apparent restriction of passion could involve just that notion of manhood. Maybe I had become like the people who find it difficult to trust the Father God or the daddy God because they can't separate Him from earthly dads who haven't been good to them? Now I'd had a good dad, but I hadn't had long-lasting beneficial partners in my life. It didn't help that I'd blocked myself off from others and that I had starved anything resembling strong emotions. I just tucked them in and hid them, pretending they weren't there.

After my last divorce I rummaged through my drawers and closet and took out anything resembling even a memory of lace or anything feminine at all. I stuffed it all into a plastic tub and put it on the top shelf of my closet. It was only my cost-conscious behavior that kept me from throwing them away in the garbage. At least I thought so. I just felt done. All of it just had to stop because I couldn't allow myself to go there again. I began to wear less makeup, choose simpler clothes, and tried not to look even appealing. I didn't want to feel sexy or feminine because that may have drawn men into my life, and I knew that would bring temptation as well as confusion. So basically I kind of neutralized myself, not understanding the consequence of putting that block on my emotions.

I continued to think about God's request for me to stay passionate with Him all the time. But there just was no clear thought as to how I could go about finding something so intense. I didn't know where it was or how to get it. But the Lord said He wanted me to be passionate with Him, so on a quest I went.

I know you're probably thinking, *How hard could that be?* But it wasn't obvious to me. It had to be more far-reaching than I knew. I was also aware that God wasn't talking about anything sexual, so that took out a large part of what I'd always thought was involved with the word *passion*. The only option left to me was to start out simple, and I did. I actually looked it up in the regular dictionary. Now as you're reading this, I feel as if I should say, "Please quit laughing," but I won't. As silly as that sounds I even feel myself grinning and shaking my head. What a state I was in! What a predicament that I was so hard-pressed to even find out what true passion meant.

But when I did look it up in the dictionary, the meaning of passion was very clear, short, and to the point. It meant to be infatuated, smitten, and intensely delighted with an obsessive eagerness and zeal.

I thought about what I had already discovered about the Lord and how He works, so I knew that He had placed those words into my life for a particular reason, and it was critical for me to get this right. But I still became puzzled about why there was something in my life that should have been so easy for me to open up to, and yet it wasn't even visible to me.

Because this story is coming to a very important part of my life, I'm going to take you backward for a few minutes. It's time to let you in on a couple of things that happened to me over the course of this five-year period of transition and healing. After I met my new Christian friends, many events made it very apparent that God was with me and He was intending on staying with me through everything. So in blind faith I stepped out and began this course of travel with Him.

My new friend, who had given all the wise advice and set me out on this journey, telephoned me one day and said he had something he was supposed to tell me. This was about eight months after Husband #4 had left me, and I was in the process of my divorce. During this particular phone call he stated he didn't know why he was supposed to tell me this but that he knew he had heard from God. He stated, "Don't give your heart away." That's basically all he said. We talked for a while, and then the phone call ended.

Several months later when I was talking with a pastor friend of mine about a house he was thinking of buying, he told me that the Lord had given him something to say to me. The word was that God was going to give me the desire of my heart. That was all he said. He didn't explain anything, so I didn't ask any questions.

I've learned to be very careful about the words people say they have gotten from God, and I think that's wise. I've gotten into the habit of waiting on the Holy Spirit to let me know if the words are something to accept or ignore, and when that peaceful acceptance comes, I tuck it right into my heart. I also write it down as soon as

I can because I don't want to forget when it came and who it came from, and of course, as much of the exact wording as possible. It would be normal to question what these words might mean to you, but for an answer as to whether they're really from God and really for you, comes in that peaceful knowing. Praying over the words given to you and asking the Holy Spirit to guide you into a confirmation will indicate whether they're from God to you. Its peace that puts to rest all the nagging doubts and feelings that something just isn't right. My theory is that if you have doubts about the words people say they have for you from God, pray over it. If you still have doubts, I would say you should put the note away for a short time, but if your doubts don't leave, throw it away and get it out of your thoughts. I've found that sometimes well-meaning people think they've heard from the Lord, but in reality it may be just something that came into their thoughts because they want to help. In my point of view, if you feel you just aren't sure either way, put it safely away, and if it really was for you, the Lord will keep bringing it back to your heart.

What I haven't yet explained is that during my life I'd had two secret desires of my heart. One desire was to be in a ministry involving music, and one was to have a faithful and godly husband. You've read about my life, so it should be easy for you to figure out that I had pretty much given up on the godly husband thing before I'd even started this journey. It wasn't that I thought the Lord had let me down. But I knew life had let me down, and I had let myself down. But the hidden yearning and those desires never really left me, even though I had tucked them way deep inside.

So in thinking about what my pastor friend had just said to me about God giving me the desire of my heart, I didn't know which desire He was talking about. To be honest, I assumed it was my desire to be involved in music. But based upon the first statement about not giving my heart away and now this statement regarding the desire of my heart, I had a fleeting, secret hope that the desire could be about a future godly man. But I was not even close at that time to being able to feel trust or love. I hadn't yet understood that because God is capable of anything, that means even fixing me.

It would take close to another year before the present pastor of my church gave me the same type of message. The Lord had definitely opened the door for me in regard to singing, and I'd been involved with the church worship team and was now in the trio with my sister and my niece. So at a combined church service on New Year's Eve, my pastor gave me the same word from the Lord while he was praying over me. He stated the Lord had told him that He was giving me my heart's desire. He also said that because God knew I didn't like to be alone, He wouldn't leave me alone. That night he also said that I would be so busy I'd have to prioritize my life. Now I was excited, and I felt sure that my pastor was talking about my desire to have a godly husband. But the message didn't really say that. It had said that God wouldn't leave me alone. So was it God who was to be my husband and bring about my heart's desire? After all, hadn't my new friend said that God could be to me what I needed him to be?

So I walked away that night full of hope and excitement but totally confused. I don't know how God talks to other people and what words He gives to them, but to me I get short, straight facts and no more. It's not audible, but it's as if I can hear a mental thought and it's not in my head voice. I know that it sounds odd and probably really difficult to figure out, but it's the truth.

From the very beginning of this journey all those things my new Christian friend said and the words that were spoken over me just made me dig deep for answers. I guess you'd say God's got my number because I've always loved investigating situations, and He knows that because He put that inside of me. So when the Holy Spirit gives me bits and pieces, He knows I'll search until I get the answer.

Approximately six months after that prayer on New Year's Eve, my pastor friend who had given me my original word about the desire of my heart walked up to me at a service. He stood in front of me and asked if I remembered when he had given that first word over me. When I said yes, he looked up at me and said the Lord had instructed him at that time to just give me the message and not say who or what it was about. But this day he had been released to go ahead and tell me, it was indeed about a godly man. This was now the third time this word about the desire of my heart had been spoken. So now I knew without a doubt who and what those spoken words concerned.

This set about in me a really big urge to continue my search in how to get closer to the Lord. I wanted to get the real meaning of letting Him be to me what I needed Him to be, and I needed to continue to try to pull myself together.

Being kicked around and kicking yourself around doesn't help you mend. It helps you hide. How many people ever actually get someone who speaks into their lives and then has others confirm again and again that the very God in heaven had made a personal promise to you? I should have been walking on air, jumping up and down, just awestruck that God was fulfilling that desire for me, but no, not me, not the old me.

Even while I was feeling joyful about the promise God had just made, I could still sense that old ugly feeling coming on strong. It was that feeling of not having enough of me left intact to be able to respect and trust a husband. I wasn't sure even then that I could be trusted to not judge this person for the behavior of past men. Actually I need to say to you that I hadn't ever voiced that before, not even in my own head. I'd really never had the thought that I made other men pay the price for the deeds of others. I'd always challenged those few men who had spoken that and believed they had said it as an excuse. But apparently I knew I had, and now I had just admitted it to myself.

All the fearful thoughts ran through my head, and the memories of my bad choices were right there in front of me. I was trying to convince myself that I couldn't be trusted to know who was right for me and who would be wrong. I was concerned that the enemy would bring in a counterfeit and I would be confused as to whether this was God's man. To think it was possible I would miss and choose wrongly was overwhelming me.

I had been learning a lot about God, and I was purposefully pursuing Him. I had talked myself into believing that would automatically help me become well emotionally. My faith seemed to be at an all-time high, or so I had thought until I began to realize it was only high in expectation for others. My past, my emotions, and my deep feelings weren't even close to being repaired and healed. In fact, I didn't know it then, but I had no real conception of that as even a possibility. I vividly remember that when people would talk about faith and healing, my mind would immediately go to thoughts about a particular person. But my thoughts never came around to me. They always deferred to someone else.

There was one particular area of my life that had caused a lot of extra pain and struggle for me, and it was mostly due to my own disappointment in myself. I knew that I could be stronger. I knew that I wasn't dumb or unwilling or unable, and yet somehow I had been and still was. That anger at myself and my disappointment was self-defeating. I continually looked back at that young, blue-eyed, blonde girl and hated that I couldn't be her and that I had let myself go in a different direction and then lost my way.

At least six months after my pastor friend had told me my desire was definitely about a man, our church had a guest speaker. After the main portion of the service they asked for people to come forward so they could pray over everyone. People lined up across the altar area, and the speaker, his wife, and all of our pastors and elders began praying for people. It was our associate pastor who prayed over me. I had never talked with him about my situation. Nor had I explained about any words spoken over me, and I had certainly never mentioned a desire for a godly husband. I guess I had been rather quiet about it … just in case. But this night he told me that the Lord had said to him that He would bring me the desire of my heart if I would stay passionate with Him. That was the start of my quest for passion. This was now the fourth time a pastor had said this, but this was the only pastor who had added a tagline. God had put a condition on it.

Chapter
39

Resting before Restoration

I had become so thoroughly happy about the changes that were going on within me that I forgot to be careful to not go backward. I think most of us at one time or another earnestly put all our efforts into something, but our intentions get all askew and out of kilter. Although you may not recognize it then, you end up doing it wrong. I thought my healing was something that would come about through learning and trusting and doing. It was never my preconceived intention to work my way through this, as if I were the one doing it, but that's exactly what I began to do. I had given the Lord permission to openly reveal to me the ugliness and the impact it had, but again I was still trying to do it myself. Oh yes, I was very used to performing it as a work and taking care of my own business. "For it is by grace you have been saved, through faith — and this is not from yourselves, it is the gift of God—not by works, so that no one can boast" (Ephesians 2:8–9 NIV).

I was well aware of the seriousness of the adverse environment I had lived. I was also aware of the consequential results of rejection from past relationships as well as from myself. What I didn't understand was how deeply my flawed decisions and resulting choices had intertwined themselves into the aspects of my life. As the Lord began this healing, so many things were brought before me. I was overwhelmed with the belief that I'd been blessed. God hadn't chosen to take that stuff and expose it to me all at one time.

When I was right in the middle of what I'll call my education of God, versus myself, my emotions were just all over the place. But one day my pastor asked if I would consider teaching a life group. Now a life group is basically the same as a Bible study, but this one was just for women. I was thrilled. I had never imagined my pastor would have enough faith in me to allow me to lead other women and share with them what I had found through the Word and with God. I had some recognition that a portion of my life had been healed and that the Lord was beginning a new healing, and this one involved my past, that one healing I'd never even considered for my own self. I had considered it for other people, yes, but for me it wasn't even on my radar until the Lord showed me it was something He wanted to do.

Even though I was excited to lead the group, I wondered how effective this would be in actuality. I always believed that for teachers to teach, they had to have a very good understanding of what they were presenting. Little did I know how much I was going to learn from my own study. I'd read and I'd research. I'd prepare the lesson, and then I'd read it again. What I wasn't equipped to know was how much the Holy Spirit would reveal to me as I taught that study. It's quite possible I could say I was my best student. In looking back, I have to smile because I am totally confident that God used this women's group as a huge stepping stone. This step helped me walk toward my future ministry and also toward the healing of my past.

I'd like to add that I would eventually come to know how much my pastor was being used by God in regard to my life. That was a comforting thought. He'd heard from God about the desire of my heart, and he'd listened to the Holy Spirit's prompting in relation to trusting me to lead that group of women. He became one of the very few people I learned to trust during that time in my life.

Even though this life group was phenomenal, it really brought out the fact that I was still very much in need of a spiritual surgery. Gaining knowledge and receiving small healings combined with changes are wonderful, but sometimes something really deep has to be removed to allow that life wound to totally heal.

When the Lord is operating and removing those hurts in your heart and the devastation that's tucked deep inside of your person, you need to prepare yourself for the amount of ugly stuff that'll be exposed. It's almost like the programs you watch on television that depict the patient in between life and death, hovering above the operating table. As the patient, you listen and watch as the surgeon removes injured and diseased matter. In the physical world surgery is bloody and an affront to the body. But for the believer, Christ has already shed His blood for you, and He's already taken the pain on the cross. The residual effect of this spiritual surgery is more of a relief, a liberation, and even a reprieve. God carefully wraps all the cleaned-out wounds with love, comfort, and peace, and He gives you the assurance that He's in charge and you're in His care.

Years of manipulation, abandonment, abuse, remorse, and sorrow were all hidden in the core of my heart. Who would have known that my self-treatment of tucking, hiding, and stuffing would cause such anger and resentment? Who knew those things would sit under my conscious level, seething and bubbling? Sometimes people go through an entire life of being angry and depressed and never get it fixed. I'm so grateful my God had the patience to hang in there with me and pull out all that junk that I carried. He was again cementing the fact that He would never leave me or forsake me, no matter, no matter what.

It was during that time of healing that I sat in on my pastor's sermon about rest. I viewed it as a simple subject. I thought to myself that as many times as I'd heard it, I was pretty sure I knew exactly what it was about. I'd read Scriptures about resting in God. To me it sounded as if you were supposed to rest after you worked to accomplish the goal because you were done. With one accomplishment at a time, you rested in between to gather up energy for the next feat. So it pretty much went in one ear and out the other. How was I supposed to know that this word *rest* would come back to me at least three more times?

God can be so amusing, and He has quite a good sense of humor. He created it, you know. He's got your number, and He knows your personality as well as your stubbornness to open your mind to new thoughts. But He's also patient, so He gives you words and phrases and Scriptures a little at a time. It's kind of like having little baby bombs dropped on you. Later the Holy Spirit gathers it all back up and presents it before you when you're more inclined to receive it. I've learned that although I take the Bible very literally, I never want it to be so literal that I don't allow the wisdom of the Holy Spirit to be able to weave Himself into it.

During a time in my life when I had received the good news of a promise from God, I was also in prayer for my older sister, who was in serious health. Every Scripture on faith and healing I'd ever jotted down was available to me. I went through all the motions, the same ones you turn to when worried almost to death about your loved ones. I did everything I knew how to do. I tried to be strong for the family and for her and tried my best to give them a blueprint of faith. You do the best you can for them because you want so desperately to give them life in your words and actions.

Three separate times, with those same pastors who spoke over me concerning the desire of my heart, each one saying to me that the Lord wanted me to rest. The pastor who was my friend spoke those words the first time, and when he did, I felt as if my head was spinning. As soon as he said it, I thought, *I can't rest. I have to do everything I can. I don't have time to rest*, and I didn't rest.

The second time it was my pastor who said it to me. I hadn't been able to go to church because I was in charge of my sister's care at that time, but with the help of family, that day I went. I found that I was extremely emotional and exceedingly tired physically and mentally. My pastor walked up to me, and without any other word, he said that the Lord had told him to tell me that I should rest.

It didn't feel as if the Lord was telling me to take physical time to rest, and since the situation hadn't changed, I knew it wasn't about it being over and resting for the next round. So I did my favorite thing, I tucked it in and went on with my business, figuring eventually I'd seek out what he'd meant.

Several weeks later my associate pastor spoke to me. He asked if I was okay and then said something was on his mind, and when I asked him what it was, he said the Lord had told him to tell me to rest, just rest.

For some reason these pastors gave me the message about rest in the same order that they had come to me about the desire of my heart. I've never discovered if there was a tie-in or if it just happened that way, but maybe if it was intentional, the Lord will share this secret with me someday. Having each of these pastors tell me the same thing would probably sound excessive under normal circumstances, but I began to imagine that quite possibly this was going to be something very important for me to figure out.

One Sunday morning months later while I was sitting in church, I finally got a piece of it. It was one of those *Aha* moments. It's difficult to explain, but it was as if the Holy Spirit just dropped a thought into my head and out popped a whole series of questions at the same time. For example, why did God rest after the six days of creating? He is God, and He never tires, so why would He need to rest? If it wasn't a physical rest, what made it important? What happens, and what does it accomplish? What's the purpose?

But yet again I found myself making it into a *work*. I didn't yet know how not to make it be a work. I've always liked investigating and figuring out problems and determining why things work the way they do. For my brain to be able to accept it, I was making it into a thing, a thing to figure out and a thing to do. Boy, there were times when I was sure the Lord had His hands full with me. But He always came through, and He always somehow helped me eventually grasp it.

I totally believe that all Scriptures in the Bible are there for some particular reason relating to how God wants you to think, pray, and behave. So apparently it was important for me to rest since He uses Himself in the second chapter of the Bible as an example. But it didn't take too long before I was certain that I had only gotten a tiny bit of what that aha moment was going to be in my life. By this time you would have thought I'd have already gotten through my head the fact that God is very thorough. When He plants a seed, you need to let it grow. You must water it and allow it to come into harvest in its own time.

Was it possible the Lord was trying to get across to me that everyone needs time for physical replenishing and recouping? Wasn't it then also possible that He wanted you to understand that this would be when He could bring a calming and a center back into the structure of your emotional output? Could it be allowing God to do what He does best, be God? What if you could let go of your control and be willing to open yourself up and let Him offer to you a new sense of direction and purpose during that rest time? Maybe it means you're giving Him all your cares, all your sorrows, all your decisions, all your time, all your healings, and then you take your hands away and trust Him with the outcome. Maybe it's you believing in Him to not only take all your hopes and worries but to work them out for your good. Maybe it's relaxing in the knowledge that He is who He says He is. Maybe it's knowing that you can pray over your situation, place it in His arms, and identify that He accepted it and He'll bring the answer. Maybe it's just standing there in full armor, knowing that He's got you and that whatever the answer is, you're completely convinced it'll be God's best. Maybe it's also just letting go and resting peacefully.

In my opinion all of that is a form of His rest. I know God so wanted to take my sadness and distress. He certainly didn't want for me to be weary in body and soul, but I was trying to do it all through the faith that I could gather up. What He wanted was to have me give to Him my absolute trust and allow Him to make whatever decision was best for the person involved. My Lord wanted me to tell Him I trusted Him, and He wanted to know I believed in Him without doubt. He wanted me to let go, taking my hands off and releasing the situation, only unto Him.

When I finally did that, wow, how empowering! It revitalized and soothed my soul and gave me a satisfaction beyond anything I could imagine. Only then did I really rest. "Come to me, all you who are weary and burdened, and I will give you rest. Take my yoke upon you and learn from me, for I am gentle and humble in heart, and you will find rest for your souls" (Matthew 11:28–29 NIV).

His intention is for you to do what you've been instructed to do through Scripture, such as putting on your armor, praying in faith, and giving Him all of your cares and burdens. It's not His design that your life be filled up with works. After all, what can you really spiritually change? Instead, stand in faith and rest in the fact that God's the one who can actually perform it.

I'd developed into someone so deeply entrenched in control I'd become convinced that in order to have strong faith and authority, I couldn't bend. But the Lord was teaching me that this wasn't bending. It was just His way. Tell Him when you need help and then mentally sit in His lap or at His feet or just beside Him and let it all out. Let yourself be comforted and then rest in the knowledge that He's got you covered.

All throughout this trial with my sister, the Lord was attempting to teach me the importance of resisting the temptation to be overwhelmed, feel caught, be disheartened, and suffer angst because of the uncertainty. God is not the enemy, and He doesn't cause disease and sickness. In fact, Christ loved you so much that He took all of that on the cross. He did that so you wouldn't have to bear it. It's this ugly, sinful, contaminated world combined with the spiritual influence of the enemy that's the major contributor for sickness, sorrows, pain, and grief.

All during that time God was at work in my life, using this experience to help develop my character and strength and to provide a more intense and profound knowledge about Him. Just as in the physical world, spiritually you have to learn to live right and get on top of your emotions and just go for what you know. Surrender your fear, fleshly desires, and pain. Let go of any bitterness and focus on Christ. He's your reservoir that you can continually draw on without any fear of ever coming up empty.

Most Christians will never hear an audible word from God. Generally He speaks through the Holy Spirit, who lives inside of every believer. The Holy Spirit gives you thoughts and ideas, and some are strong enough you think that if you closed your eyes, you could actually see the words. He has a love so strong for you that when you get quiet before Him, you can actually feel it.

If that's never happened to you and you want it, find somewhere with no distractions. I find my shower is a good place where my body as well as my heart and mind can get clean. Close your eyes and just ask the Lord for His forgiveness for any sin you've committed, no matter how big or how little. Tell the Lord how much you love Him and need Him. If there's a particular area you need help with, open up and begin to talk with Him about it. If you want to cry, just cry. This is definitely the place and the time. Ask Him for help, discernment and wisdom, about future decisions and just lay your heart open. Just be with Him and let Him be with you. You'll probably end up feeling almost brand new, as if you've done a spring housecleaning. It's really like clearing out and letting go of all the junk, taking a deep breath, and then having someone hug you.

If you have never asked the Lord into your life to be your Savior but you'd like to, I want to offer this portion of Scripture and add a prayer for you to read out loud.

John 3:16 (NIV) says, "For God so loved the world that he gave his one and only Son, that whoever believes in him shall not perish but have eternal life" (John 3:16 NIV).

You can recite the following prayer: "Father God, I come to You in the name of Jesus, believing He is Your only begotten Son. I recognize that He gave His life and shed His blood on the cross so that I might be saved. I confess my sins to You and ask with a repentant heart for Your forgiveness. I love You and want to be with You forever. In the name of Jesus. Amen."

If you've at one time been saved but you're not living the way you should and you want to make it right with the Lord, just repeat that same prayer and then add on to it anything your heart wants to say to Him. Our God is a God of second, third, fourth, and fifth chances! It's never too late with Him as long as you're alive. Remember—He never forsakes you, and His love never changes, no matter, no matter what! God bless you.

Chapter
40

Oh, How He Loves Me

So what is it that brings to you the hope that you can actually have the desires of your heart? How can you be so hopeful through the damage collected? Will you be able to face what you'll be presented with in order to have that life-changing event? What is it inside of you that would allow you to believe you can have that new beginning?

In God's request for me to stay passionate with Him, I began to realize this request meant that I would have to do more than just embrace the relationship between the Lord and me. The Lord was showing to me that I also needed to include the desire of my heart, a godly husband.

However, I felt the Lord wasn't going to fulfill that desire until I could fully grasp this concept of unrelenting passion and lastly liberate myself of my need to control. I knew the Lord was aware of why I'd lived with a controlling manner and that it involved my need to self-protect. My internal defense was based on occurrences throughout my adult life. For me to be passionate and develop into a woman who could surrender to the leading of a godly man, I would have to give up my control. I would have to be willing to be led.

I'd spent years of living life, believing I could only count on myself. I'd been proud of the fact that it wasn't necessary to have a man in my life to take care of me financially, and I knew if I had to, I could live life alone. To most people, God's request for a release of control might not be a huge problem; however, for me it was difficult at best. The fact that it took more than eighteen months of getting me to fully understand that just proves my own point. I was deeply embedded. Of course the Lord knew me thoroughly and therefore knew my why, but He also knew I wouldn't be able to slip into the footsteps of a wife with that protective mode still intact.

Every time I thought I had it figured out, I'd find the Lord wanted more. It eventually dawned on me that this was going to happen until He finally had me where I needed to be. As strange as all this was, I knew if I could get it together, it was going to be very freeing, and I'd get my passionate, godly husband out of it.

While I was digging around, trying to find out anything that made sense, I came across a new discovery I didn't like. I found a glitch in my personality that I believe brought about the appearance of complacency. Now the word *complacent* generally means a feeling of being satisfied, smug, selfish, or self-righteous. It's as if everything is okay for you and you don't have to go out of your way or do anything different. It gives off a feeling of satisfaction and doesn't encourage being energetic. But if you laid my personality open flat for all to see, you wouldn't find that version of complacency. I did care, and I wasn't smug. My casual, offhanded way of dealing with stuff wasn't because I was satisfied or self-righteous. It was my own way of hiding and pretending that all was fine. When situations got too tough, too close to home, or too involved, or when they caused me to have to be too bold, I would tuck in and hide, wearing my brave face. I certainly wasn't aware that it made me appear like I didn't care because in truth I probably cared too much.

Wow, another newly revealed flaw in my character. I didn't want people to view me like this. So I began praying that the Lord would give me additional confidence in myself and a realization of what not to do in this regard. I didn't want to tuck in and hide anymore, and I certainly didn't want people to think I was a stuck-up and indifferent individual.

In this manual there have been several occasions when I sat back and wondered about me. How did I get so messed up? Was I more messed up than most people? If it could happen to me, could it happen to other well-intentioned people? I can only give praise to the Lord for allowing me so many chances to get it right. No one on earth would ever allow me as many chances as God. He's my daddy God, who loves me unconditionally, and He's the initiator of my rest and restoration. He takes all lost things, including you and me, and brings them back to life.

The healing of my emotional past and harsh memories was a lengthy process, but every day I realize those memories that come back to me don't hold any pain. Gaining self-confidence and slowly losing my grip on independence and self-control is causing me to take periodic looks at myself. God is so good. He gifts to you the ability to learn from the Holy Spirit in a way that He worked out just for you. Through each move forward, there came a new reward, a new benefit. God has been continually developing in me an intentional goal of a future and a hope to concentrate and focus on. Each day it's a more defined journey, and it brings me closer to the prize.

I'd known that God's request to me about staying passionate with Him was super important. It had been right up there in my thoughts, never leaving me. It and what it meant to me was what drove me to my desire to become a caring, loving, lively, agreeable, and vibrant woman.

I realized I was becoming easier on myself and less afraid of how people saw me. I'd always been harsh on myself because of my lack of confidence and my insistence on assuming guilt. But the ugly enemy's thoughts were losing their edge. The more I began to understand how much Jesus loved me, the more loved I felt, and the more love I felt, the more love I found I could give. I was becoming passionate, and the truth is that I was actually understanding what it meant. It seemed the more I knew of God's love for me, the deeper in love with Him I became, and my trust of Him was solid and sure.

My new Christian friend had been right. Finding out how much Jesus loved me was what I'd needed to find. Jesus had filled every area of my life and had been to me whatever I'd asked and needed Him to be. I'd called on Him to protect me, guard me, and guide me as a husband would, and He'd never once let me down.

It all seemed so simple back then as a teenager, lying on the sofa that night, crying in the dark with my heart laid totally open to the Lord, asking for an answer to my prayer. I'd prayed without regard for anything else other than an answer of whether or not that young man in my life was to be my future husband. God's answer left no doubt in my mind that he was not my God-picked future, and He was telling me I could let him go. "'For I know the plans I have for you,' declares the LORD, 'plans to prosper you and not to harm you, plans to give you hope and a future'" (Jeremiah 29:11 NIV).

Right now, even as I'm writing these last sentences, my mind has wandered into a question. Was God now fulfilling my original desire to have in my life a man He had picked as a godly husband for me? Was God wiping away more than forty years of wrong choices and frustration and sorrows by bringing to me now the person who would totally fit me right where I'm at? Was God honoring my original prayer of faith because this was the first time I had allowed Him the opportunity to do so? I can only wonder, but I tell you that it's a thrilling thought. You know, God is exactly like that. He always connects everything, and He never leaves anything out. My heart is somehow telling me that's exactly what He's doing for me. It's as if He's bringing it all back around in a circle so that it will be as if nothing has ever been missing or broken.

I know my heart's desire is only steps away. I had to be ready, healed, compliant to the Lord, and passionately passionate. When my man comes, I'll be ready for Him as my husband, partner, friend, and team leader!

Right now as I'm putting together these last sentences, I remember what was given to me as a word from God on that New Year's Eve service. I remember my pastor telling me God was saying He knew I didn't like to be alone. Right now in my remembrance of that, I get chills when I realize how well my God knows me and all my internal and deep-seated emotions. I can only imagine the person He has handpicked just for me. "Before I formed you in the womb I knew you, before you were born I set you apart" (Jeremiah 1:5 NIV).

He made me. Of course He knows me. He counts the hairs on my head. Of course He knows me. He sets me under His feathers and protects me with His wings. Of course He knows me!

Not the End!

Printed in the United States
By Bookmasters